THE SHAKESPEARE PARALLEL TEXT SERIES, THIRD EDITION

Julius Cæsar

by William Shakespeare

Perfection Learning© Corporation
Logan, Iowa 51546-0500

Editorial Director	Julie A. Schumacher
Senior Editor	Rebecca Christian
Series Editor	Rebecca Burke
Editorial Assistant	Kate Winzenburg
Writer, Modern Version	Wim Coleman
Design Director	Randy Messer
Design	Mark Hagenberg
Production	PerfecType
Art Research	Laura Wells
Cover Art	Brad Holland

© 2004 **Perfection Learning© Corporation**
1000 North Second Avenue, P.O. Box 500
Logan, Iowa 51546-0500
Tel: 1-800-831-4190 • Fax: 1-800-543-2745

Printed in the United States of America.

Paperback ISBN 0-7891-6083-8
Cover Craft ISBN 0-7569-1491-4
2 3 4 5 6 PP 07 06 05 04

TABLE OF CONTENTS

SHAKESPEARE'S TIMES:
THE QUESTION OF SUCCESSION

Why did William Shakespeare decide to set a tragedy in ancient Rome? Paradoxically, Shakespeare may have written about the past because of

Julius Caesar (100–44 B.C.), Roman statesman and general

what was happening in his present. Queen Elizabeth I had come to power because the king had no male heir. She was popular, but also old and childless. Her subjects were concerned about who would succeed her. Some were even ready to depose her (just as some Romans had been ready to overthrow Julius Caesar).

Plots to overthrow the queen defied the common belief that God appointed sovereigns. According to the doctrine of divine right, subjects had no right to change rulers. Among her enemies was the charismatic Earl of Essex, who believed that it was time for a strong, young king—like himself—to take the throne. Essex was eventually beheaded for treason.

The story of Julius Caesar also had striking parallels to the politics of Shakespeare's time. Like Brutus and Caesar, Essex and Elizabeth had once been close friends. Like Brutus, Essex invoked honor and patriotism to support his arguments. Like Brutus, Essex was willing to shed blood to achieve his goals. Finally, the question of succession was a burning issue in both eras.

Of course, there were also significant differences between England and Rome. For one, the Romans had to choose between two forms of government: a republic or an absolute ruler. The English simply had to identify a new monarch. These differences allowed Shakespeare to write about contemporary politics without personal risk.

Julius Caesar was first performed in 1599, the midpoint of Shakespeare's career. The play can be thought of as either a history or tragedy. Like most tragedies, it describes the pride and fall

Actor playing Marcus Junius Brutus (85–42 B.C.), Roman statesman

of powerful people. Like most histories, it has no clear-cut villain, so it is open to interpretation. During some periods, the murder of Caesar has been seen as justified; during others, it has been considered treason.

With this history-tragedy, Shakespeare began moving into his great tragic themes. In his book *Shakespeare*, Anthony Burgess says that the playwright became preoccupied with "the puzzle of the good intention that could produce evil . . . . Brutus was a murderer, but still the noblest Roman of them all. The conscience of the killer was to become an obsessive theme in the tragedies Shakespeare was preparing to write."

Why was Shakespeare suddenly fascinated with evil? We may never know, for Shakespeare's life remains a mystery.

SHAKESPEARE'S ROME:
THE STRUGGLE FOR POWER

Julius Caesar on his throne

Julius Caesar dramatizes the struggle to control Rome after Caesar's assassination. Both Shakespeare and his Elizabethan audience knew who finally won. They also had no trouble understanding references to Roman beliefs and customs. However, most people today need more historical background than Shakespeare provides.

Kings ruled Rome for many years. Rome's last king was the tyrant Tarquin, an evil man who abused his power.

The Republic developed a government of many levels, each with its particular duties. Power was kept in the hands of the **patricians**—those from old noble families—and wealthy middle-class citizens. Working-class citizens—called **plebeians**—were represented in government but had little actual power. Slaves, foreigners, and women were not allowed to hold office or vote.

The highest-ranking officials in the Roman Republic were two **consuls**, who presided over the Senate and all elections. Caesar first became a consul in 59 B.C.

The consuls selected the members of the **Senate**—Rome's ruling body. The Senate's decrees became law unless vetoed by the **tribunes**.

The ten tribunes were the only plebeians who were elected officials. In theory, the tribunes could check the power of the senators and protect the rights of ordinary citizens. They had the power to veto Senate decrees. Tribunes were also by law immune from arrest. This prevented the aristocrats from silencing a tribune by throwing him in jail. Consequently, many tribunes were assassinated when they stood in the way of a senator's ambition.

Mark Antony before the crowds

The Republic was certainly not a democracy and was not without its problems. The patricians spent a lot of time fighting among themselves, each trying to get just a little more power. During times of crisis, a powerful man could become dictator.

Despite these problems, more people had a voice in the government than ever before. By the time Julius Caesar was born, Rome looked down on any nation ruled by a monarch. Most citizens swore that Rome would never have another king. However, by 44 B.C., many Romans were convinced that the ambitions of one man threatened their Republic.

SHAKESPEARE'S SOURCES

Shakespeare based *Julius Caesar* on written accounts of Roman history, especially Plutarch's *Lives of the Noble Greeks and Romans*. Shakespeare may also have been familiar with *Lives of the Caesars*, a collection of biographies written by Gaius Tranquillus Suetonius (70–140 A.D.), a secretary to Emperor Hadrian. Nevertheless, Shakespeare changed many historical facts to fit his fictional play. The "real" Julius Caesar (100–44 B.C.) first became popular as the official responsible for putting on combats with wild beasts and gladiators. He joined with Pompey and Crassus in the First **Triumvirate**—a form of government in which power is controlled by three people. As his fame as a brilliant military general grew, so did his own power.

Caesar defeated Pompey and his followers in the Battle of Pharsalus in 48 B.C. Caesar then returned to Rome. By 46 B.C., he had been named dictator for life.

Fears of his ambition grew with the arrival of Cleopatra in Rome. Caesar had met the Queen of Egypt in 48 B.C. She and Caesar fell in love and had a child. The Romans knew that Cleopatra was a charming and ambitious woman who wanted Caesar to become king and take her as his queen. They hated the idea of having to bow before Caesar and his foreign queen.

In 44 B.C., Caesar was killed by his best friend, Brutus, and others. The assassins claimed that they wanted to preserve the Roman Republic. Ironically, the struggle for power after Caesar's death led to the birth of the Roman Empire. Mark Antony (83–30 B.C.), who had also been one of Caesar's best friends, became a great general, popular with both the army and the Roman people. After Caesar's death, Antony took advantage of the chaos to ally himself with

Richard Chamberlain as Octavius Caesar, Commonwealth United production, 1970

Caesar's heir, Octavius, and another general, Lepidus. With his allies, Antony defeated Brutus and Cassius at the Battle of Philippi. The Second Triumvirate ruled ruthlessly, killing hundreds of political enemies. After a quarrel with Octavius, Antony joined forces with Cleopatra of Egypt. The two attempted to overthrow Octavius, but they were defeated at the Battle of Actium in 31 B.C. Antony and Cleopatra committed suicide, and Octavius became the sole ruler of Rome.

Timeline

509 B.C.   Lucius Junius Brutus rebels against the brutal tyrant Tarquin the Proud and establishes the Roman Republic.

202 B.C.   Rome defeats Carthage in the Second Punic War and becomes a major military power.

100 B.C.   Julius Caesar is born.

82 B.C.   Lucius Cornelius Sulla becomes dictator of Rome. Sulla plans to have Caesar assassinated as part of a purge. Caesar flees Rome. Sulla later relents, and Caesar returns.

65 B.C.   Caesar gains popularity as *aedile*, or director of public works and games, by putting on combats with wild beasts and gladiators.

63 B.C.   Caesar is elected *pontifex maximus*, head of the state religion.

60 B.C.   The First Triumvirate (Caesar, Pompey, and Crassus) rules Rome.

59 B.C.   Caesar is elected consul, one of Rome's two executive officers, in a fixed election. He marries Calphurnia. Julia, Caesar's daughter by his first marriage, weds Pompey.

55 B.C.   Caesar invades Germany and leads military expedition to Britain.

54 B.C.   Julia dies, and tension grows between Caesar and Pompey; Caesar invades Britain again.

51 B.C.   Caesar completes his conquest of Gaul.

49 B.C.   Caesar refuses Pompey's order to give up his army and begins civil war. He appoints himself tribune for life and dictator.

48 B.C.	Caesar falls in love with Cleopatra and defeats Pompey's army at Pharsalus. (He pardons Brutus and Cassius, who fought against him, and appoints them to high office.)
45 B.C.	Caesar becomes the only ruler of the Roman Republic.
44 B.C.	Caesar is named dictator for life (February);
	Caesar refuses crown offered by Mark Antony (March);
	Caesar plans to lead an army to avenge the defeat of Crassus (March);
	Caesar is assassinated (March);
	Antony forms the Second Triumvirate with Octavius and Lepidus.
43 B.C.	Cicero is among the 300 senators and 2,000 businessmen who die by order of the Second Triumvirate.
42 B.C.	Brutus and Cassius commit suicide after Antony defeats them at Philippi.
41 B.C.	Antony joins forces with Cleopatra; they plan to rule new Roman Empire.
31 B.C.	Octavian defeats Antony at Actium; Antony and Cleopatra commit suicide and Octavian becomes sole ruler of Rome.
27 B.C.	Octavian becomes the first Roman Emperor.

READING JULIUS CAESAR

USING THIS PARALLEL TEXT

This edition of *Julius Caesar* is especially designed for readers who aren't familiar with Shakespeare. If you're fairly comfortable with his language, simply read the original text on the left-hand page. When you come to a confusing word or passage, refer to the modern English version on the right or the footnotes at the bottom.

If you think Elizabethan English doesn't even sound like English, read a passage of the modern version silently. Then read the same passage of the original. You'll find that Shakespeare's language begins to come alive for you. You may choose to work your way through the entire play this way.

As you read more, you'll probably find yourself using the modern version less and less. Remember, the parallel version is meant to be an aid, not a substitute for the original. If you read only the modern version, you'll cheat yourself out of Shakespeare's language—his quick-witted puns, sharp-tongued insults, and mood-making images.

Keep in mind that language is a living thing, constantly growing and changing. New words are invented and new definitions for old words are added. Since Shakespeare wrote over four hundred years ago, it is not surprising that his work seems challenging to today's readers.

Here are some other reading strategies that can increase your enjoyment of the play.

BACKGROUND

Knowing some historical background makes it easier to understand what's going on. In addition to the timeline, you will find information about Shakespeare's life and Elizabethan theater at the back of the book. Reading the summaries that precede each act will also help you to follow the action of the play.

GETTING THE BEAT

Like most dramatists of his time, Shakespeare frequently used **blank verse** in his plays. In blank verse, the text is written in measured lines that do not rhyme. Look at the following example from *Julius Caesar*.

> Let's carve him as a dish fit for the gods,
> Not hew him as a carcass fit for hounds.
> And let our hearts, as subtle masters do,
> Stir up their servants to an act of rage . . .

You can see that the four lines above are approximately equal in length, but they do not cover the whole width of the page as the lines in a story or essay might. They are, in fact, unrhymed verse with each line containing ten or eleven syllables. Furthermore, the ten syllables can be divided into five sections, called **iambs**, or feet. Each iamb contains one unstressed (U) and one stressed (/) syllable. Try reading the lines below, giving emphasis to the capitalized syllable in each iamb.

U /	U /	U /	U /	U /
Let's CARVE	him AS	a DISH	fit FOR	the GODS,

U /	U /	U /	U /	U /
Not HEW	him AS	a CAR	cass FIT	for HOUNDS.

The length of a line of verse is measured by counting the stresses. This length is known as the **meter**, and when there are five stresses and the rhythm follows an unstressed/stressed pattern, it is known as **iambic pentameter**. Much of Shakespeare's work is written in iambic pentameter.

Of course, Shakespeare was not rigid about this format. He sometimes varied the lines by putting accents in unusual places, by having lines with more or fewer than ten syllables, and by varying where pauses occur. An actor's interpretation can also add variety. (Only a terrible actor would deliver lines in a way that makes the rhythm sound singsong!)

Courtyard of a Roman palace

PROSE

In addition to verse, Shakespeare wrote speeches in **prose**, or language without rhythmic structure. Look at Act III, Scene ii, lines 242–245 ("Why, friends, you go to do you know not what . . ."), where Antony speaks to the Plebeians. Try beating out the rhythm of Antony's speech, and you will find that it usually follows the pattern of iambic pentameter. But if you try to impose the same rhythm on the Plebeians' speeches that follow, you'll discover that it doesn't work at all. Shakespeare generally uses prose for comic speeches, to show madness, and for characters of lower social rank such as servants. His upper-class characters generally do not speak in prose. But these weren't hard-and-fast rules as far as Shakespeare was concerned. Whether characters speak in verse or prose is often a function of the situation and whom they're addressing, as well as their social status.

CONTRACTIONS

As you know, contractions are words that have been combined by substituting an apostrophe for a letter or letters that have been removed. Contractions were as common in Shakespeare's time as they are today. For example, we use *it's* as a contraction for the words *it is*. In Shakespeare's writing you will discover that *'tis* means the same thing. Shakespeare often used the apostrophe to shorten words so that they would fit into the rhythmic pattern of a line. This is especially true of verbs ending in -ed. Note that in Shakespeare's plays, the -ed at the end of a verb is usually pronounced as a separate syllable. Therefore, *walked* would be pronounced as two syllables, *walk*ed*, while *walk'd* would be only one.

SPEAK AND LISTEN

Remember that plays are written to be acted, not read silently. Reading aloud—whether in a group or alone—helps you to "hear" the meaning. Listening to another reader will also help. You might also enjoy listening to a recording of the play by professional actors.

CLUES AND CUES

Shakespeare was sparing in his use of stage directions. In fact, many of those in modern editions were added by later editors. Added stage directions are usually indicated by brackets. For example, [aside] tells the actor to give the audience information that the other characters can't hear. Sometimes a character's actions are suggested by the lines themselves.

THE PLAY'S THE THING

Finally, if you can't figure out every word in the play, don't get discouraged. The people in Shakespeare's audience couldn't either. At that time, language was changing rapidly and standardized spelling, punctuation, grammar, and even dictionaries did not exist. Besides, Shakespeare loved to play with words. He made up new combinations, like *fat-guts* and *mumble-news*. To make matters worse, the actors probably spoke very rapidly. But the audience didn't strain to catch every word. They went to a Shakespeare play for the same reasons we go to a movie—to get caught up in the story and the acting, to have a great laugh, or a good cry.

⊕ ⊕ ⊕

Cast of Characters

Caesar and his supporters

JULIUS CAESAR
CALPHURNIA his wife
MARK ANTONY ⎫
OCTAVIUS CAESAR ⎬ The ruling Triumvirate after Caesar's death
LEPIDUS ⎭

The conspirators against Caesar

Conspirators

BRUTUS	**CASCA**	**CINNA**	**METELLUS CIMBER**
CAIUS CASSIUS	**DECIUS BRUTUS**	**TREBONIUS**	**CAIUS LIGARIUS**

Family and followers

PORTIA Brutus's wife
LUCIUS Brutus's boy servant
CLAUDIO
LABEO* ⎫
FLAVIUS* ⎬ Personal followers of Brutus
CLITUS
STRATO
DARDANUS ⎭

VARRUS
PINDARUS Cassius's slave
LUCILIUS
TITINIUS ⎫
MESSALA ⎬ Officers of Brutus and Cassius
YOUNG CATO
VOLUMNIUS
STATILIUS* ⎭

Other Romans

CICERO ⎫
PUBLIUS CIMBER ⎬ Senators
POPILIUS LENA
OTHER SENATORS* ⎭

FLAVIUS ⎫ Tribunes critical
MARULLUS ⎭ of Caesar
SOOTHSAYER ⎫ Who try to
ARTEMIDORUS ⎭ warn Caesar
SERVANTS TO
   CAESAR, ANTONY, AND OCTAVIUS

CINNA THE POET
A CYNIC POET
1ST, 2ND, 3RD, 4TH PLEBEIANS
CARPENTER
COBBLER
MESSENGER
1ST, 2ND, 3RD SOLDIERS
OTHER PLEBEIANS*

* nonspeaking parts

JULIUS CAESAR

ACT I

Louis Calhern (far left), as Julius Caesar, and James Mason (far right), as Brutus, listen to the Soothsayer's warning. Joseph L. Mankiewicz director, 1953

"BEWARE THE IDES OF MARCH."

Before You Read

1. Do you think that positive political change can ever be brought about through violence? Explain your answer.

2. As you read, consider how Caesar is characterized by others as well as by his own comments and actions.

Literary Elements

1. A **pun** is a play on words with similar sounds but more than one spelling or meaning. In Act I, Scene i of *Julius Caesar*, the cobbler says he is "a mender of bad soles," referring not only to the soles of shoes but also to the spiritual force that some think distinguishes humans from animals.

2. **Foreshadowing** refers to hints in the text about what will occur later in the plot. In the second scene of the play you are about to read, a soothsayer, or fortune-teller, warns: "Beware the ides of March." Because the "ides" were the 15th day of the month, we can expect something bad to happen in the play on March 15.

3. A **simile** is a comparison of two unlike things using *like* or *as*. In Act I, Cassius uses a simile that shows Caesar's power over others: "Why, man, he doth bestride the narrow world / Like a Colossus, and we petty men / Walk under his huge legs and peep about / To find ourselves dishonorable graves."

4. **Conflict** is what creates tension and drama in literature. **External conflict** refers to a struggle between humans and an outside force such as nature or another individual. In *Julius Caesar*, conflict exists between the ordinary citizens and those who plot to kill Caesar. **Internal conflict** refers to a mental struggle within the individual. Portia's love for her husband clashes with her anger at being kept from his secret plans.

Words to Know

The following vocabulary words appear in Act I in the original text of Shakespeare's play. However, they are words that are still commonly used. Read the definitions here and pay attention to the words as you read the play (they will be in boldfaced type).

chafing	resisting; showing irritation
cogitations	ideas; thoughts
concave	curved in; hollowed inward
conjure	to imagine or make up
construe	interpret; take to mean
encompassed	contained; included
fawn	to flatter in order to receive favors
incenses	angers; enrages
infirmity	illness; sickness
ingratitude	ungratefulness; thanklessness
lamented	expressed grief or sorrow for
portentous	meaningful; ominous
redress	make right; remedy
servile	slavish; subservient

Act Summary

The people of Rome are on holiday, rejoicing at Julius Caesar's victory over his rival Pompey. Two tribunes, Marullus and Flavius, ask some tradesmen why the commoners are not working and get riddles for an answer. The tribunes accuse the mob of being fickle. They had supported Pompey until recently, but now they are happy to see Caesar as the leader of the Republic.

Caesar has come out to watch the spectacles of Lupercal, a feast day. A soothsayer warns the great man to beware the ides of March (the middle day, or 15th on the old Roman calendar). Caesar sends him away, annoyed, before continuing through the crowd.

Left alone, Brutus and Cassius speak in a roundabout way of Caesar's pride and ambition. For fear of committing treason, neither man is able

Julian Glover as Cassius (left), and John Nettles as Brutus (right),
Sir Peter Hall, director, Barbican Theatre, 1996

to speak freely of his envy and suspicions. So they verbally dance around the subject of Caesar's quest for absolute power.

As Caesar passes by again, he is struck by the "lean and hungry look" of Cassius. He notes that men who "think too much . . . are dangerous" before proceeding on. Brutus asks Casca, a learned senator who appears to be a friend of Caesar, why the people have been cheering. Casca replies that Mark Antony has offered Caesar the crown of Rome three times, and each time Caesar has turned it down. The senators are irked by the people's eagerness to make Caesar king and unimpressed by his show of humility. Brutus promises to get back to Cassius about the matters left unspoken in their earlier conversation.

A month later, it is the night before the ides of March. Casca and Cicero discuss the unnatural events of the stormy night. Cicero is not convinced by Casca's superstitions, but he admits that the empire seems to be in a state of disorder. He departs.

Cassius arrives and hints that the storm-tossed night reminds him of a man who would also bring Rome down with him. Casca reports that the Senate may be preparing to appoint Caesar king. Both he and Cassius admit their hatred of Caesar and fierce desire to get rid of him. They decide that any conspiracy must include Brutus, who has the power to betray them as well as to help them succeed. Cassius sends Casca to deliver letters to Brutus that will help convince their powerful friend of the popularity of their cause.

ACT I, SCENE I

[*Rome. A street.*] *Enter* FLAVIUS, MARULLUS, *and certain* COMMONERS *over the stage.*

FLAVIUS
Hence! Home, you idle creatures, get you home.
Is this a holiday? What, know you not,
Being mechanical, you ought not walk
Upon a laboring day without the sign
5 Of your profession?—Speak, what trade art thou?

CARPENTER
Why, sir, a carpenter.

MARULLUS
Where is thy leather apron and thy rule?
What dost thou with thy best apparel on?—
You, sir, what trade are you?

COBBLER
10 Truly, sir, in respect of a fine workman, I am but, as you
would say, a cobbler.

MARULLUS
But what trade art thou? Answer me directly.

COBBLER
A trade, sir, that I hope I may use with a safe conscience,
which is indeed, sir, a mender of bad soles.

MARULLUS
15 What trade, thou knave? Thou naughty knave, what trade?

COBBLER
Nay, I beseech you, sir, be not out with me; yet if you be
out, sir, I can mend you.

MARULLUS
What mean'st thou by that? Mend me, thou saucy fellow?

COBBLER
Why, sir, cobble you.

ACT 1, SCENE 1

Rome. A street. FLAVIUS, MARULLUS, *and several* COMMONERS *enter from different sides of the stage.*

FLAVIUS
Go away! Go home, you lazy creatures, go on home!
Is this a holiday? Why, don't you know that,
because you are common laborers, you shouldn't go out
on a workday except
in your working clothes? Tell me, what trade do you practice?   5

CARPENTER
Why, I'm a carpenter, sir.

MARULLUS
Where is your leather apron and your ruler?
What are you doing, dressed in your best clothes?
You, sir—what trade do *you* practice.

COBBLER
To be honest, sir—compared to a skilled workman, I am only   10
what you might call a cobbler.

MARULLUS
But what trade do you practice? Answer me straightforwardly.

COBBLER
A trade, sir, that I hope I can practice with a good conscience;
indeed, sir, I am a mender of bad soles.

FLAVIUS
What trade, you rascal? You worthless rascal, what trade?   15

COBBLER
No, I beg you sir, don't fall out with me; and yet, if you fall out,
I can mend you.

MARULLUS
What do you mean by that? Mend me, you insolent fellow?

COBBLER
Why, sir, fix your shoes.

FLAVIUS

20 Thou are a cobbler, art thou?

COBBLER

Truly, sir, all that I live by is with the awl. I meddle with
no tradesman's matters nor women's matter; but withal*
I am indeed, sir, a surgeon to old shoes. When they are in
great danger, I recover* them. As proper men as ever trod
25 upon neat's leather have gone upon my handiwork.

FLAVIUS

But wherefore art not in thy shop today?
Why dost thou lead these men about the streets?

COBBLER

Truly, sir, to wear out their shoes, to get myself into more
work. But indeed, sir, we make holiday to see Caesar and
30 to rejoice in his triumph.

MARULLUS

Wherefore rejoice? What conquest brings he home?
What tributaries follow him to Rome
To grace in captive bonds his chariot wheels?
You blocks, you stones, you worse than senseless things!
35 O you hard hearts, you cruel men of Rome,
Knew you not Pompey?* Many a time and oft
Have you climbed up to walls and battlements,
To towers and windows, yea, to chimney tops,
Your infants in your arms, and there have sat
40 The livelong day, with patient expectation,
To see great Pompey pass the streets of Rome.
And when you saw his chariot but appear,
Have you not made an universal shout,
That Tiber trembled underneath her banks
45 To hear the replication of your sounds
Made in her **concave** shores?
And do you now put on your best attire?

---

22 *withal* wordplay on "with awl," "with all," and "withal" (which means
"nevertheless")

24 *recover* wordplay on "re-sole" and "make well"

36 *Pompey* Pompey the Great, who was defeated by Caesar in civil war in 48 B.C.
and later murdered

FLAVIUS

So you're a cobbler, are you?   20

COBBLER

Indeed, sir—everything I earn is by the awl. I don't fool around
with labor politics or with women. But nevertheless, I am
indeed, sir, a doctor to old shoes; when they are in great danger,
I mend them. The most respectable men who have ever walked
in cattle hide have worn my handiwork.   25

FLAVIUS

But why aren't you in your shop today?
Why are you leading these men through the streets?

COBBLER

To be honest, sir, to wear out their shoes and get myself more
work. But seriously, sir—we're taking a holiday to see Caesar
and to rejoice in his triumphal parade.   30

MARULLUS

Why should you rejoice? What prizes has he brought home?
Do any tribute-paying prisoners follow him to Rome
to decorate his chariot wheels in chains of captivity?
You blocks, you stones, you worse than unfeeling things!
Oh, you hard-hearted, cruel men of Rome—   35
don't you remember Pompey? Often—many times—
you have climbed up walls and battlements
to towers and windows—why, all the way to chimney tops—
carrying your babies in your arms; and there you have sat
the whole day through, waiting patiently   40
to see great Pompey pass through the streets of Rome.
And as soon as you saw his chariot appear,
didn't you shout in one great voice,
until the Tiber trembled within her banks
to hear the echo that your shouting caused   45
between her overhanging shores?
And now, do you put on your best clothes?

And do you now cull out a holiday?
And do you now strew flowers in his way
50   That comes in triumph over Pompey's blood?
Be gone!
Run to your houses, fall upon your knees,
Pray to the gods to intermit the plague
That needs must light on this **ingratitude**.

FLAVIUS

55   Go, go, good countrymen, and for this fault
Assemble all the poor men of your sort;
Draw them to Tiber banks, and weep your tears
Into the channel, till the lowest stream
Do kiss the most exalted shores of all.

Exeunt all the COMMONERS.

60   See whe'er their basest mettle be not moved;
They vanish tongue-tied in their guiltiness.
Go you down that way towards the Capitol.
This way will I. Disrobe the images,
If you do find them decked with ceremonies.

MARULLUS

65   May we do so?
You know it is the feast of Lupercal.*

FLAVIUS

It is no matter; let no images
Be hung with Caesar's trophies. I'll about
And drive away the vulgar from the streets.
70   So do you too, where you perceive them thick.
These growing feathers plucked from Caesar's wing
Will make him fly an ordinary pitch,
Who else would soar above the view of men
And keep us all in **servile** fearfulness.

Exeunt.

---

66   *feast of Lupercal* an ancient Roman fertility festival held on February 15 in honor
of Lupercus, an Italian equivalent of the god Pan

And now, do you decide to turn a working day into a holiday?
And now, do you scatter flowers along the path
of the man who comes as the conqueror of Pompey's sons? 50
Go away!
Run to your houses, fall upon your knees,
and pray to the gods to hold back the plague
that surely must be your punishment for such ingratitude.

FLAVIUS

Go, go, good countrymen—and to atone for this sin, 55
gather together all the poor men of your sort.
Lead them down to the banks of the Tiber, then weep your tears
into the stream until the water rises to its highest banks,
even if the tide is at its lowest.

All the COMMONERS *exit.*

Look at how even the lowest man among them is touched; 60
they slip away, tongue-tied with guilt.
You go that way to the Capitol,
and I'll go this way. If you find any statues covered
with ornaments, remove them.

MARULLUS

May we do so? 65
You know it is the feast of Lupercal.

FLAVIUS

It doesn't matter. Let no statues
be draped with anything honoring Caesar. I'll go around
driving the common people from the streets;
you do so, too, wherever you find them gathered. 70
By plucking these growing feathers from Caesar's wing,
we'll make him fly to an ordinary height;
otherwise, he will soar beyond men's sight
and keep us all subservient and fearful.

They exit in different directions.

ACT I, SCENE II

[*Rome. A public place.*] *Enter* CAESAR, ANTONY
(*for the course**), CALPHURNIA, PORTIA, DECIUS,
CICERO, BRUTUS, CASSIUS, CASCA, *a*
SOOTHSAYER, [*and* CITIZENS]. *After them,*
MARULLUS *and* FLAVIUS.

CAESAR
Calphurnia.

CASCA
                  Peace, ho! Caesar speaks.

CAESAR
                                      Calphurnia.

CALPHURNIA
Here, my lord.

CAESAR
5 Stand you directly in Antonio's way
When he doth run his course.—Antonio.

ANTONY
Caesar, my lord.

CAESAR
Forget not in your speed, Antonio,
To touch Calphurnia; for our elders say,
10 The barren, touched in this holy chase,
Shake off their sterile curse.

ANTONY
                        I shall remember.
When Caesar says, "Do this," it is performed.

CAESAR
Set on and leave no ceremony out.

SOOTHSAYER
15 Caesar!

---

for the course Footraces were part of the celebration of the Lupercalia. Plutarch
tells us that men "run naked through the city, striking in sport them they meet in
their way with leather thongs, hair and all on, to make them give place."

ACT 1, SCENE 2

A public place in Rome. CAESAR, CALPHURNIA, PORTIA, DECIUS, CICERO, BRUTUS, CASSIUS, CASCA, and a FORTUNE-TELLER enter—along with ANTONY, who is dressed for racing. MARULLUS, FLAVIUS, and CITIZENS enter later.

CAESAR
Calphurnia.

CASCA
Quiet, everyone! Caesar speaks.

CAESAR
Calphurnia.

CALPHURNIA
I'm here, my lord.

CAESAR
Stand directly in Antony's way   5
when he runs in the race.—Antony.

ANTONY
Caesar, my lord.

CAESAR
As you run, Antony, do not forget
to touch Calphurnia; for our elders say
that infertile women will shake off the curse of sterility   10
when touched in this sacred race.

ANTONY
I shall remember.
When Caesar says, "Do this," it is done.

CAESAR
Go on and don't leave out any parts of the ceremony.

Trumpet signal.

FORTUNE-TELLER
Caesar!   15

CAESAR
Ha! Who calls?

CASCA
Bid every noise be still. Peace, yet again!

CAESAR
Who is it in the press that calls on me?
I hear a tongue shriller than all the music
20 Cry "Caesar!" Speak. Caesar is turned to hear.

SOOTHSAYER
Beware the ides of March.*

CAESAR
What man is that?

BRUTUS
A soothsayer bids you beware the ides of March.

CAESAR
Set him before me. Let me see his face.

CASSIUS
25 Fellow, come from the throng.

[*The* SOOTHSAYER *comes forward.*]

Look upon Caesar.

CAESAR
What sayst thou to me now? Speak once again.

SOOTHSAYER
Beware the ides of March.

CAESAR
He is a dreamer. Let us leave him. Pass.

Sennet. Exeunt. Brutus and Cassius remain.

CASSIUS
Will you go see the order of the course?

BRUTUS
30 Not I.

---

21 *ides of March* March 15. According to the Roman calendar, the ides were the
midpoint of the month: the fifteenth day in March, May, July, and October, and
the thirteenth day in all other months.

CAESAR
What! Who calls?

CASCA
Let every noise be still. Once again, be quiet!

CAESAR
Who is it in the crowd that calls to me?
I hear a voice, more shrill than all the music,
crying, "Caesar!" Speak. Caesar has turned to hear you.   20

FORTUNE-TELLER
Beware of March 15.

CAESAR
Who is that man?

BRUTUS
A fortune-teller tells you to beware of March 15.

CAESAR
Bring him before me. Let me see his face.

CASSIUS
Fellow, come out of the crowd.   25

The FORTUNE-TELLER *comes forward.*

Look at Caesar.

CAESAR
What did you say to me just now? Say it once again.

FORTUNE-TELLER
Beware of March 15.

CAESAR
He is a dreamer. Let us leave him. Move on.

Trumpet signal. All but BRUTUS *and* CASSIUS *exit.*

CASSIUS
Will you go see how the race is run?

BRUTUS
Not I.   30

CASSIUS

I pray you do.

BRUTUS

I am not gamesome; I do lack some part
Of that quick spirit that is in Antony.
Let me not hinder, Cassius, your desires.
35   I'll leave you.

CASSIUS

Brutus, I do observe you now of late.
I have not from your eyes that gentleness
And show of love as I was wont to have.
You bear too stubborn and too strange a hand
40   Over your friend that loves you.

BRUTUS

                      Cassius,
Be not deceived. If I have veiled my look,
I turn the trouble of my countenance
Merely upon myself. Vexed I am
45   Of late with passions of some difference,
Conceptions only proper to myself,
Which give some soil, perhaps, to my behaviors.
But let not therefore my good friends be grieved
(Among which number, Cassius, be you one)
50   Nor **construe** any further my neglect
Than that poor Brutus, with himself at war,
Forgets the shows of love to other men.

CASSIUS

Then, Brutus, I have much mistook your passion,
By means whereof this breast of mine hath buried
55   Thoughts of great value, worthy **cogitations**.
Tell me, good Brutus, can you see your face?

BRUTUS

No, Cassius, for the eye sees not itself
But by reflection, by some other things.

CASSIUS

'Tis just.
60   And it is very much **lamented**, Brutus,
That you have no such mirrors as will turn

CASSIUS

I beg you to do so.

BRUTUS

I'm not interested in sports. I lack some
of that lively spirit that can be found in Antony.
Don't let me keep you from what you want to do, Cassius.
I'll leave you.   35

CASSIUS

Brutus, I've been watching you lately.
I've not seen in your eyes that courtesy
and display of love that I'm accustomed to receive from you.
You hold too harsh and unfriendly a hand
against me—your friend who loves you.   40

BRUTUS

Cassius,
don't misunderstand. If I have seemed distant,
it's because I've been turning my troubled expression
entirely toward myself. Lately, I've been
vexed by some conflicting emotions,   45
issues that are strictly personal,
which perhaps have put a stain on my behavior.
But I don't want this to grieve my good friends—
of which number you are one, Cassius—
nor should you make anything more of my neglect   50
than that Brutus is at war with himself,
and forgets to show love to other men.

CASSIUS

Then I have greatly misinterpreted your feelings, Brutus,
and because of that, I've kept buried in my breast
thoughts of great value, important considerations.   55
Tell me, good Brutus—can you see your face?

BRUTUS

No, Cassius, for the eye cannot see itself
unless reflected by some other thing.

CASSIUS

That's true.
And it's very regrettable, Brutus,   60
that you have no such mirror to show

Your hidden worthiness into your eye,
That you might see your shadow. I have heard
Where many of the best respect in Rome—
65 Except immortal Caesar—speaking of Brutus,
And groaning underneath this age's yoke,
Have wished that noble Brutus had his eyes.

BRUTUS
Into what dangers would you lead me, Cassius,
That you would have me seek into myself
70 For that which is not in me?

CASSIUS
Therefore, good Brutus, be prepared to hear.
And since you know you cannot see yourself
So well as by reflection, I, your glass,
Will modestly discover to yourself
75 That of yourself which you yet know not of.
And be not jealous on me, gentle Brutus.
Were I a common laughter, or did use
To stale with ordinary oaths my love
To every new protester; if you know
80 That I do **fawn** on men and hug them hard,
And after scandal them; or if you know
That I profess myself in banqueting
To all the rout, then hold me dangerous.

Flourish and shout.

BRUTUS
What means this shouting?
85 I do fear the people choose Caesar
For their king.

CASSIUS
Ay, do you fear it?
Then must I think you would not have it so.

BRUTUS
I would not, Cassius, yet I love him well.
90 But wherefore do you hold me here so long?
What is it that you would impart to me?
If it be aught toward the general good,

your hidden worthiness to your own eye,
so you could see your reflection. I have heard
many of the most reputable men in Rome—
except immortal Caesar—groan   65
underneath the yoke of our time, and speak of Brutus,
wishing that he could see himself through their eyes.

BRUTUS
What dangers do you wish to lead me into, Cassius—
since you want me to seek in myself
qualities that aren't in me?   70

CASSIUS
As for that, good Brutus, prepare to listen.
And since you know that you cannot see yourself
except by reflection, I will be your mirror,
and show you—without exaggerating—things
that you do not yet know about yourself.   75
And don't be suspicious of me, noble Brutus.
If I were a laughingstock, or if I often
cheapened myself by frequent promises of love
to each new person who called himself my friend; or if you knew
me to flatter men and embrace them tightly,   80
then later slander them; or if you knew
me to profess my friendships at parties
to the vulgar crowd, then you could consider me dangerous.

Fanfare and a shout from the crowd.

BRUTUS
What does this shouting mean? I am afraid that the people
have chosen Caesar to be their king.   85

CASSIUS
Indeed, do you fear it?
Then I can't help thinking you don't want it to be so.

BRUTUS
I don't want it, Cassius, and yet I love him well.
But why are you keeping me here so long?   90
What is it that you wish to tell me?
If it has anything to do with the public welfare,

Set honor in one eye and death i' th' other,
And I will look on both indifferently;
95 For let the gods so speed me as I love
The name of honor more than I fear death.

CASSIUS
I know that virtue to be in you, Brutus,
As well as I do know your outward favor.
Well, honor is the subject of my story.
100 I cannot tell what you and other men
Think of this life; but, for my single self,
I had as lief not be as live to be
In awe of such a thing as I myself.
I was born free as Caesar, so were you;
105 We both have fed as well, and we can both
Endure the winter's cold as well as he.
For once, upon a raw and gusty day,
The troubled Tiber **chafing** with her shores,
Caesar said to me, "Dar'st thou, Cassius, now
110 Leap in with me into this angry flood
And swim to yonder point?" Upon the word,
Accoutred as I was, I plunged in
And bade him follow; so indeed he did.
The torrent roared, and we did buffet it
115 With lusty sinews, throwing it aside
And stemming it with hearts of controversy.
But ere we could arrive the point proposed,
Caesar cried, "Help me, Cassius, or I sink!"
I, as Aeneas,* our great ancestor,
120 Did from the flames of Troy upon his shoulder
The old Anchises* bear, so from the waves of Tiber
Did I the tired Caesar. And this man
Is now become a god, and Cassius is
A wretched creature and must bend his body
125 If Caesar carelessly but nod on him.
He had a fever when he was in Spain,
And when the fit was on him, I did mark
How he did shake. 'Tis true, this god did shake.

---

119 *Aeneas* legendary founder of the Roman state and hero of Virgil's *Aeneid*

121 *Anchises* father of Aeneas

put honor before one of my eyes and death before the other,
and I will look on them both impartially;
let the gods make me prosper only if I love   95
honor more than I fear death.

CASSIUS
I know that you've got that virtue inside you, Brutus,
as surely as I know your outward appearance.
Well, honor is the subject of my story.
I don't know what you and other men   100
think of this life; but as for myself alone,
I would just as soon be dead as live
in awe of another human being like myself.
I was born as free as Caesar, and so were you;
we both have enjoyed the same pleasures as he, and we   105
    can both
endure the winter's cold as well as he.
Once, on a rough and windy day,
when the waves of the turbulent Tiber dashed against her
    shores,
Caesar said to me, "Cassius, do you dare
to leap with me now into this angry current   110
and swim to that point over there?" As soon as he said this—
although I was fully clothed—I plunged right in
and told him to follow. So indeed, he did.
The water rushed along, and we fought against it
with vigorous might, throwing it aside   115
and swimming against it with competitive hearts.
But before we could arrive at the point agreed to,
Caesar cried, "Help me, Cassius, or I'll sink!"
So just as Aeneas, our great ancestor,
carried old Anchises out of the flames of Troy   120
on his shoulder, I pulled the tired Caesar
out of the waves of the Tiber. And this man
has now become a god, and Cassius is
a pathetic creature who must bow deeply
if Caesar merely gives him a passing nod.   125
He had a fever when he was in Spain,
and when he had a seizure, I noticed
how he shook. It's true—this god really shook.

His coward lips did from their color fly,
130　And that same eye, whose bend doth awe the world,
Did lose his luster. I did hear him groan.
Ay, and that tongue of his that bade the Romans
Mark him and write his speeches in their books,
"Alas!" it cried, "Give me some drink, Titinius,"
135　As a sick girl. Ye gods, it doth amaze me
A man of such a feeble temper should
So get the start of the majestic world
And bear the palm alone.

　　　Shout. Flourish.

BRUTUS
Another general shout?
140　I do believe that these applauses are
For some new honors that are heaped on Caesar.

CASSIUS
Why, man, he doth bestride the narrow world
Like a Colossus,* and we petty men
Walk under his huge legs and peep about
145　To find ourselves dishonorable graves.
Men at some time are masters of their fates.
The fault, dear Brutus, is not in our stars,*
But in ourselves, that we are underlings.
"Brutus" and "Caesar"—what should be in that "Caesar"?
150　Why should that name be sounded more than yours?
Write them together: yours is as fair a name.
Sound them: it doth become the mouth as well.
Weigh them: it is as heavy. **Conjure** with 'em:
"Brutus" will start a spirit as soon as "Caesar."
155　Now, in the names of all the gods at once,
Upon what meat doth this our Caesar feed
That he is grown so great? Age, thou art shamed.
Rome, thou hast lost the breed of noble bloods.
When went there by an age, since the great flood,*

143　*Colossus* a bronze statue of Apollo as the sun god, more than 100 feet high,
whose legs are said to have spanned the harbor of Rhodes

147　*stars* According to widely held astrological beliefs, the position of the stars (used
generally for any heavenly body) governed, or at least reflected, the affairs of men.

His cowardly lips lost all their color,
and that same eye whose glance keeps the world in awe   130
lost its gleam. I heard him groan.
Yes, that tongue of his that has commanded the Romans
to listen to him and write his speeches in their notebooks
cried out, "Alas! Give me some drink, Titinius,"
just like a sick girl. Oh you gods, it astounds me   135
that a man of such a weak constitution
should outdistance everyone else in this grand world
and carry off the victor's prize all by himself.

> *A shout from the crowd. Fanfare.*

BRUTUS

Everyone shouted again.
I believe that all this applause   140
is for some new honors that have been heaped on Caesar.

CASSIUS

Why, man, he straddles the narrow world
like a Colossus, and we lesser men
walk under his huge legs and peep about,
looking for graves suitable to our lowliness.   145
But at some time or other, men can be masters of their fates.
Dear Brutus, it's not the fault of our stars,
but of ourselves that we are underlings.
"Brutus" and "Caesar"—what is it about that name "Caesar"?
Why should that name be more famous than yours?   150
Write them side by side: yours is just as pleasant a name.
Say them both: yours suits the mouth just as well.
Weigh them both: yours is as heavy. Cast a spell with them:
"Brutus" will summon a spirit as quickly as "Caesar" does.
Now—in the names of all the gods at once—   155
what food does this Caesar of ours eat
that has made him grow so great? This age should be
    ashamed!
Rome, you have stopped breeding spirited men!
When, since the great flood, has an age gone by

---

159   *the great flood* an early, mythical flood in which Zeus destroyed all of corrupt
       mankind except Deucalion and his wife Pyrrha

160   But it was famed with more than with one man?
When could they say, till now, that talked of Rome,
That her wide walks **encompassed** but one man?
Now it is Rome indeed, and room* enough,
When there is in it but one only man.
165   O, you and I have heard our fathers say
There was a Brutus* once that would have brooked
Th' eternal devil to keep his state in Rome
As easily as a king.

BRUTUS
    That you do love me, I am nothing jealous.
170   What you would work me to, I have some aim.
How I have thought of this, and of these times,
I shall recount hereafter. For this present,
I would not so—with love I might entreat you—
Be any further moved. What you have said,
175   I will consider; what you have to say,
I will with patience hear, and find a time
Both meet to hear and answer such high things.
Till then, my noble friend, chew upon this:
Brutus had rather be a villager
180   Than to repute himself a son of Rome
Under these hard conditions as this time
Is like to lay upon us.

CASSIUS
    I am glad that my weak words
Have struck but thus much show of fire from Brutus.

Enter CAESAR *and his* TRAIN.

BRUTUS
185   The games are done, and Caesar is returning.

---

163   *Rome . . . room* In Shakespeare's time, "Rome" and "room" were pronounced alike.

166   *Brutus* Lucius Junius Brutus, who drove the Tarquins out of Rome and
established the Roman Republic in 509 B.C. Marcus Brutus claimed to be
descended from him.

that wasn't celebrated for more than one man? 160
When, before now, could it be said of Rome
that her wide streets held only one notable man?
Now it is Rome, indeed—and a room is enough
when there is only one man in it.
Oh, you and I have heard our fathers say 165
that there was once a Brutus who would have allowed
the devil himself to hold power in Rome
before he'd let a king do so.

BRUTUS

That you love me, I do not doubt.
I have some idea of what you want to persuade me of. 170
Later on, I shall tell you my own thoughts
about this matter and these times. For the time being
—if I may ask this as a friend—I do not wish
to be urged any further. What you have said,
I'll consider; whatever else you have to say, 175
I'll listen to it with patience and find a proper
time to fully discuss such great affairs.
Till then, my noble friend, consider this:
Brutus would rather be a common villager
than to call himself a son of Rome 180
under the hard conditions that this time
is likely to cause for us.

CASSIUS

I am glad
that my weak words have stirred at least this much of a sign
of fire in Brutus.

> CAESAR *and his* FOLLOWERS *enter.*

BRUTUS

The games are over, and Caesar is returning. 185

CASSIUS

As they pass by, pluck Casca by the sleeve,
And he will, after his sour fashion, tell you
What hath proceeded worthy note today.

BRUTUS

I will do so. But look you, Cassius,
190 The angry spot doth glow on Caesar's brow,
And all the rest look like a chidden train.
Calphurnia's cheek is pale, and Cicero
Looks with such ferret and such fiery eyes
As we have seen him in the Capitol,
195 Being crossed in conference by some senators.

CASSIUS

Casca will tell us what the matter is.

CAESAR

Antonio.

ANTONY

Caesar.

CAESAR

Let me have men about me that are fat,
200 Sleek-headed men, and such as sleep a-nights.
Yond Cassius has a lean and hungry look.
He thinks too much. Such men are dangerous.

ANTONY

Fear him not, Caesar, he's not dangerous.
He is a noble Roman, and well given.

CAESAR

205 Would he were fatter! But I fear him not.
Yet if my name were liable to fear,
I do not know the man I should avoid
So soon as that spare Cassius. He reads much,
He is a great observer, and he looks
210 Quite through the deeds of men. He loves no plays,
As thou dost, Antony; he hears no music.
Seldom he smiles, and smiles in such a sort
As if he mocked himself, and scorned his spirit
That could be moved to smile at anything.

CASSIUS

As they pass by, tug Casca by the sleeve;
in his sour way, he'll tell you
whatever has happened today that is worth knowing about.

BRUTUS

I will do so. But look, Cassius—
there's a hint of anger in Caesar's expression,   190
and all of his followers look like they've been scolded.
Calphurnia's cheeks are pale, and Cicero's
eyes are as fiery red as a ferret's—
just as we have seen him in the Capitol
when he's been contradicted in debate by some senators.   195

CASSIUS

Casca will tell us what the matter is.

CAESAR

Antony.

ANTONY

Caesar.

CAESAR

Let me have men around me who are fat—
men with smoothly combed hair who sleep well at night.   200
Cassius over there is lean and hungry-looking.
He thinks too much. Such men are dangerous.

ANTONY

Don't be afraid of him, Caesar; he's not dangerous.
He is a noble Roman and of a good disposition.

CAESAR

If only he were fatter! But I'm not afraid of him.   205
Still, if it were possible for the man called Caesar to be afraid,
I do not know of a man I would avoid
more surely than that skinny Cassius. He reads a great deal,
he is a great observer, and he understands
men's hidden motives. He does not love plays,   210
as you do, Antony; he does not listen to music.
He seldom smiles, and when he does, he seems
to mock himself and despise his spirit
because it can be moved to smile at anything.

215 Such men as he be never at heart's ease
Whiles they behold a greater than themselves,
And therefore are they very dangerous.
I rather tell thee what is to be feared
Than what I fear; for always I am Caesar.
220 Come on my right hand, for this ear is deaf,
And tell me truly what thou think'st of him.

Sennet. Exeunt CAESAR *and his* TRAIN.

[CASCA *remains behind.*]

CASCA
You pulled me by the cloak. Would you speak with me?

BRUTUS
Ay, Casca, tell us what hath chanced today
That Caesar looks so sad.

CASCA
225 Why, you were with him, were you not?

BRUTUS
I should not then ask Casca what had chanced.

CASCA
Why, there was a crown offered him; and, being offered
him, he put it by with the back of his hand, thus, and
then the people fell a-shouting.

BRUTUS
230 What was the second noise for?

CASCA
Why, for that too.

CASSIUS
They shouted thrice. What was the last cry for?

CASCA
Why, for that too.

BRUTUS
Was the crown offered him thrice?

CASCA
235 Ay, marry, was 't, and he put it by thrice, every time gentler
than other; and at every putting-by mine honest neighbors
shouted.

Such men are never at ease in their hearts 215
as long as they look on someone greater than themselves,
and so they are very dangerous.
But I tell you what ought to be feared,
and not what I fear; for I am always Caesar.
Come around to my right side, for I am deaf in this ear, 220
and tell me what you really think about him.

> *Trumpet signal.* CAESAR *and his* FOLLOWERS *exit, but* CASCA
> *remains behind.*

CASCA
You tugged me by the cloak. Do you want to speak with me?

BRUTUS
Yes, Casca. Tell us what happened today
that made Caesar look so serious.

CASCA
Why, you were with him, weren't you? 225

BRUTUS
If I were, I wouldn't ask Casca what had happened.

CASCA
Why, a crown was offered to him, and when it was offered to
him, he pushed it aside with the back of his hand—like this—
and then the people started shouting.

BRUTUS
What was the second shouting about? 230

CASCA
Why, for the same thing.

CASSIUS
They shouted three times. What was the last shout for?

CASCA
Why, for the same thing.

BRUTUS
Was the crown offered to him three times?

CASCA
Yes, indeed, it was, and he pushed it aside three times—every 235
time more reluctantly than the last—and every time he
pushed it away, my honest neighbors shouted.

CASSIUS
Who offered him the crown?

CASCA
Why, Antony.

BRUTUS
240   Tell us the manner of it, gentle Casca.

CASCA
I can as well be hanged as tell the manner of it. It was
mere foolery; I did not mark it. I saw Mark Antony offer
him a crown—yet 'twas not a crown neither, 'twas one of
these coronets—and, as I told you, he put it by once; but
245   for all that, to my thinking he would fain have had it.
Then he offered it to him again; then he put it by again;
but to my thinking, he was very loath to lay his fingers off
it. And then he offered it the third time. He put it the
third time by, and still as he refused it, the rabblement
250   hooted and clapped their chopt hands, and threw up
their sweaty nightcaps, and uttered such a deal of stinking
breath because Caesar refused the crown that it had
almost choked Caesar, for he swounded and fell down at
it. And for mine own part, I durst not laugh, for fear of
255   opening my lips and receiving the bad air.

CASSIUS
But soft, I pray you. What, did Caesar swound?

CASCA
He fell down in the marketplace and foamed at the
mouth and was speechless.

BRUTUS
'Tis very like he hath the falling sickness.*

CASSIUS
260   No, Caesar hath it not; but you and I
And honest Casca, we have the falling sickness.

CASCA
I know not what you mean by that, but I am sure Caesar
fell down. If the tag-rag people did not clap him and hiss

---

259   *falling sickness* In the next lines Cassius turns "falling sickness" into a political
metaphor for willing subjection.

CASSIUS
Who offered him the crown?

CASCA
Why, Antony.

BRUTUS
Tell us how it happened, gentle Casca. 240

CASCA
I can just as easily be hanged as tell how it happened. It was mere foolery; I paid no attention to it. I saw Mark Antony offer him a crown—yet it was not a crown, either; it was one of those coronets. And as I told you, he pushed it aside once. But even so, it seemed to me that he would rather have taken it. 245
Then Antony offered it to him again; then he pushed it aside again; but it seemed to me that he was very unhappy to take his fingers off it. And then Antony offered it a third time, and he pushed it aside a third time; and every time that he refused it, the rabble hooted, and clapped their calloused hands, and 250
threw up their sweaty woolen caps; and because Caesar refused the crown, they exhaled such a great amount of stinking breath that it almost choked Caesar, for he fainted and fell down because of it. As for myself, I didn't dare laugh for fear of opening my lips and breathing in the bad air. 255

CASSIUS
But slow down, please. Did you say that Caesar fainted?

CASCA
He fell down in the marketplace, and foamed at the mouth, and was speechless.

BRUTUS
It's quite likely that he suffers from the falling sickness.

CASSIUS
No, Caesar does not have it; but you and I 260
and honest Casca—*we* have the falling sickness.

CASCA
I don't know what you mean by that, but I am sure that Caesar fell down. The ragged mob applauded him and

him, according as he pleased and displeased them, as they
use to do the players in the theater, I am no true man.

BRUTUS
What said he when he came unto himself?

CASCA
Marry, before he fell down, when he perceived the
common herd was glad he refused the crown, he plucked
me ope his doublet and offered them his throat to cut.
And I had been a man of any occupation, if I would not
have taken him at a word, I would I might go to hell
among the rogues. And so he fell. When he came to
himself again, he said, if he had done or said anything
amiss, he desired their worships to think it was his
infirmity. Three or four wenches where I stood cried,
"Alas, good soul!" and forgave him with all their hearts.
But there's no heed to be taken of them; if Caesar had
stabbed their mothers, they would have done no less.

BRUTUS
And after that, he came thus sad away?

CASCA
Ay.

CASSIUS
Did Cicero say anything?

CASCA
Ay, he spoke Greek.

CASSIUS
To what effect?

CASCA
Nay, and I tell you that, I'll ne'er look you i' th' face again.
But those that understood him smiled at one another and
shook their heads. But for mine own part, it was Greek to
me. I could tell you more news too. Marullus and
Flavius, for pulling scarves off Caesar's images, are put to
silence. Fare you well. There was more foolery yet, if I
could remember it.

hissed him, according to whether he pleased or displeased them, just as they do with players in the theater. If they didn't, I'm no honest man. 265

BRUTUS
What did he say when he regained consciousness?

CASCA
Indeed, before he fell down, when he saw that the common herd was glad he refused the crown, he plucked open his jacket and offered them his throat to cut. If I had been one of those working men, I would have taken him at his word, or 270 may I go to hell along with all the other rogues. And so he fell. When he came to himself again, he said that if he had done or said anything he shouldn't have, he hoped those fine folks would excuse it because of his illness. Three or four women 275 where I stood cried, "Alas, good soul!" and forgave him with all their hearts. But there's no need to think anything of that; if Caesar had stabbed their mothers, they would have done no less.

BRUTUS
And after that, he came away looking so serious?

CASCA
Yes. 280

CASSIUS
Did Cicero say anything?

CASCA
Yes, he spoke Greek.

CASSIUS
What did he have to say?

CASCA
Indeed, if I were to try to tell you that, I'd never be able to look you in the face again. But those who understood him 285 smiled at one another and shook their heads. But as far as I was concerned, it was Greek to me. I could tell you more news, too: Marullus and Flavius have been put away for pulling scarves off Caesar's statues. Farewell. There was even more foolery, if I could only remember it. 290

CASSIUS

Will you sup with me tonight, Casca?

CASCA

No, I am promised forth.

CASSIUS

Will you dine with me tomorrow?

CASCA

Ay, if I be alive, and your mind hold, and your dinner
295   worth the eating.

CASSIUS

Good. I will expect you.

CASCA

Do so. Farewell both.

     Exit.

BRUTUS

What a blunt fellow is this grown to be!
He was quick mettle when he went to school.

CASSIUS

300   So is he now, in execution
Of any bold or noble enterprise,
However he puts on this tardy form.
This rudeness is a sauce to his good wit,
Which gives men stomach to digest his words
305   With better appetite.

BRUTUS

And so it is. For this time I will leave you.
Tomorrow, if you please to speak with me,
I will come home to you; or if you will,
Come home to me, and I will wait for you.

CASSIUS

310   I will do so. Till then, think of the world.

     Exit BRUTUS.

Well, Brutus, thou art noble. Yet I see
Thy honorable mettle may be wrought
From that it is disposed. Therefore it is meet

CASSIUS
Will you have supper with me tonight, Casca?

CASCA
No, I've promised to eat elsewhere.

CASSIUS
Will you have lunch with me tomorrow?

CASCA
Yes, if I'm still alive, and you don't change your mind, and your
food is worth eating.   295

CASSIUS
Good. I will expect you.

CASCA
Do so. Farewell to you both.

> *He exits.*

BRUTUS
What a coarse fellow he's become!
He had a lively spirit when he was in school.

CASSIUS
He still does, when it comes to carrying out   300
any bold or worthy enterprise,
even though he puts on a sluggish appearance.
This rough manner adds flavor to his keen intelligence,
which gives men the appetite to digest his words
with better enjoyment.   305

BRUTUS
So that's how it is. I will leave you for now.
Tomorrow, if you want to speak with me,
I will come to your house; or if you prefer,
come to my house, and I will wait for you there.

CASSIUS
I will do so. Until then, think about the current state of things.   310

> BRUTUS *exits.*

(*to himself*) Well, Brutus, you are noble. And yet I see
that your honorable character can be persuaded
away from its inclinations. For this reason, it is best

That noble minds keep ever with their likes;
315 For who so firm that cannot be seduced?
Caesar doth bear me hard, but he loves Brutus.
If I were Brutus now, and he were Cassius,
He should not humor me. I will this night,
In several hands, in at his windows throw,
320 As if they came from several citizens,
Writings, all tending to the great opinion
That Rome holds of his name, wherein obscurely
Caesar's ambition shall be glanced at.
And after this, let Caesar seat him sure,
325 For we shall shake him, or worse days endure.

Exit.

for noble minds to keep company with other noble minds,
for who is so strong-willed that he cannot be seduced?   315
Caesar resents me, but he loves Brutus.
If I were Brutus now, and Brutus were Cassius,
he wouldn't sway me as I have swayed him. Tonight
I will throw several letters into his window—
in different kinds of handwriting, so they'll seem to have come
    from different citizens;   320
they will all deal with the great opinion
that Rome holds of Brutus's name, and also
indirectly hint at Caesar's ambition.
After this, let Caesar do what he can to secure his position,
for we will shake him, or else suffer worse days.   325

    He exits.

ACT I, SCENE III

[*Rome. A street.*] *Thunder and lightning. Enter* CASCA *and* CICERO [*at different doors*].

CICERO

Good even, Casca. Brought you Caesar home?
Why are you breathless, and why stare you so?

CASCA

Are not you moved, when all the sway of earth
Shakes like a thing unfirm? O Cicero,
5   I have seen tempests when the scolding winds
Have rived the knotty oaks, and I have seen
Th' ambitious ocean swell and rage and foam,
To be exalted with the threat'ning clouds;
But never till tonight, never till now,
10 Did I go through a tempest dropping fire.
Either there is a civil strife in heaven,
Or else the world, too saucy with the gods,
Incenses them to send destruction.

CICERO

Why, saw you anything more wonderful?

CASCA

15 A common slave—you know him well by sight—
Held up his left hand, which did flame and burn
Like twenty torches joined; and yet his hand,
Not sensible of fire, remained unscorched.
Besides—I ha' not since put up my sword—
20 Against the Capitol I met a lion,
Who glazed upon me and went surly by
Without annoying me. And there were drawn
Upon a heap a hundred ghastly women,
Transformed with their fear, who swore they saw
25 Men all in fire walk up and down the streets.
And yesterday the bird of night did sit,
Even at noonday, upon the marketplace,
Hooting and shrieking. When these prodigies
Do so conjointly meet, let not men say,
30 "These are their reasons, they are natural,"

ACT 1, SCENE 3

*A street in Rome. Thunder and lightning. CASCA and CICERO
enter from separate directions.*

CICERO
Good evening, Casca. Did you escort Caesar home?
Why are you breathless, and why do you stare like that?

CASCA
Aren't you disturbed when the whole worldly order
shakes like something flimsy? Oh, Cicero,
I have seen tempests where the scolding winds   5
have split mighty oaks, and I have seen
the ambitious ocean swell, rage, and foam
until it rose as high as the threatening clouds.
But never till tonight—never till now—
have I walked through a storm that dropped fire from the sky.   10
Either there is a civil war in heaven,
or else the world, too insolent toward the gods,
has provoked them to send destruction.

CICERO
Why, have you seen anything else that was really amazing?

CASCA
A common slave—you'd know him if you saw him—   15
held up his left hand, which burst into flame and burned
like twenty torches joined together; and yet his hand
did not feel any pain and remained unscorched.
And also—I've not put my sword away since—
I met a lion near the Capitol,   20
who gazed at me, then walked sullenly by
without disturbing me. And a hundred women
who had all turned white as ghosts from fear
were huddled together in a crowd, swearing that they saw
men all on fire, walking up and down the streets.   25
And yesterday, a screech-owl sat
in the marketplace at noon,
hooting and shrieking. When such extraordinary events
happen all at once, men had better not say,
"Here are the reasons for this happening—it's all natural."   30

For I believe they are **portentous** things
Unto the climate that they point upon.

CICERO

Indeed, it is a strange-disposed time.
But men may construe things after their fashion,
35   Clean from the purpose of the things themselves.
Comes Caesar to the Capitol tomorrow?

CASCA

He doth, for he did bid Antonio
Send word to you he would be there tomorrow.

CICERO

Good night then, Casca.
40   This disturbed sky is not to walk in.

CASCA

                  Farewell, Cicero.

Exit CICERO.

Enter CASSIUS.

CASSIUS

Who's there?

CASCA

        A Roman.

CASSIUS

                Casca, by your voice.

CASCA

45   Your ear is good. Cassius, what night is this!

CASSIUS

A very pleasing night to honest men.

CASCA

Who ever knew the heavens menace so?

CASSIUS

Those that have known the earth so full of faults.
For my part, I have walked about the streets,
50   Submitting me until the perilous night,
And thus unbraced, Casca, as you see,
Have bared my bosom to the thunder-stone;

For I believe these things promise trouble
to the region where they take place.

CICERO
Indeed, it is an abnormal time.
But men can interpret things as they like
and completely miss the purpose of the things themselves.   35
Is Caesar coming to the Capitol tomorrow?

CASCA
He is, for he commanded Antony
to send word to you that he would be there tomorrow.

CICERO
Good night then, Casca. This rough weather
is not fit for walking in.   40

CASCA
Farewell, Cicero.

CICERO *exits.* CASSIUS *enters.*

CASSIUS
Who's there?

CASCA
A Roman.

CASSIUS
By your voice, I know you are Casca.

CASCA
You've got good hearing. Cassius, what a night this is!   45

CASSIUS
It's a very pleasant night for honest men.

CASCA
Who ever knew the heavens to be so menacing?

CASSIUS
Anyone who knows how full of faults the world is.
As for me, I have walked through the streets
showing myself to the threatening night—   50
and with my jacket open, Casca, as you can see,
I have bared my chest to the lightning bolt.

And when the cross blue lightning seemed to open
The breast of heaven, I did present myself
55   Even in the aim and very flash of it.

CASCA

But wherefore did you so much tempt the heavens?
It is the part of men to fear and tremble
When the most mighty gods by tokens send
Such dreadful heralds to astonish us.

CASSIUS

60   You are dull, Casca, and those sparks of life
That should be in a Roman you do want,
Or else you use not. You look pale, and gaze,
And put on fear, and cast yourself in wonder,
To see the strange impatience of the heavens,
65   But if you would consider the true cause—
Why all these fires; why all these gliding ghosts;
Why birds and beasts, from quality and kind;
Why old men, fools, and children calculate;
Why all these things change from their ordinance,
70   Their natures, and preformed faculties,
To monstrous quality—why, you shall find
That heaven hath infused them with these spirits
To make them instruments of fear and warning
Unto some monstrous state.
75   Now could I, Casca, name to thee a man
Most like this dreadful night.
That thunders, lightens, opens graves, and roars
As doth the lion in the Capitol;
A man no mightier than thyself or me
80   In personal action, yet prodigious grown,
And fearful, as these strange eruptions are.

CASCA

'Tis Caesar that you mean, is it not, Cassius?

CASSIUS

Let it be who it is. For Romans now
Have thews and limbs like to their ancestors.
85   But, woe the while, our fathers' minds are dead,
And we are governed with our mothers' spirits;
Our yoke and sufferance show us womanish.

And when the jagged blue lightning seemed to rip open
the breast of heaven, I put myself
right in the path of its flash.   55

CASCA

But why did you tempt the heavens like that?
It's proper for men to be afraid and tremble
when the mightiest gods send signs
by such dreadful messengers to stun us with fear.

CASSIUS

You are dull-witted, Casca—and either you lack   60
the wit a Roman ought to have,
or else you make no use of it. You look pale, and stare,
and show fear, and give yourself up to amazement
at seeing the strange impatience of the heavens.
But if you would consider the true reason   65
why there are all these fires and gliding ghosts;
why birds and beasts act so freakishly;
why even old men, idiots, and children are able to prophesy;
why the normal behaviors, characters,
and inborn qualities of all things have changed   70
to an unnatural condition; why, then you will realize
that heaven has put spirits into all of them
to make them instruments of fear and warning
concerning some abnormal state of affairs.
Now, Casca, I could tell you the name of a man   75
who is much like this dreadful night
that flashes and thunders, opens graves and roars
like that lion in the Capitol.
He is no mightier a man than you or me
in his personal deeds, yet he has grown menacing   80
and frightening, just like these strange outbursts of nature.

CASCA

It's Caesar that you mean, isn't it, Cassius?

CASSIUS

Let it be whoever it is. For Romans today
have muscles and limbs just like their ancestors.
But—alas for this time!—our fathers' minds are dead, 85
and we are ruled by our mothers' spirits.
Our meek surrender to servitude proves us to be womanish.

CASCA

Indeed, they say the Senators tomorrow
Mean to establish Caesar as a king,
90 And he shall wear his crown by sea and land
In every place save here in Italy.

CASSIUS

I know where I will wear this dagger then;
Cassius from bondage will deliver Cassius.
Therein, ye gods, you make the weak most strong;
95 Therein, ye gods, you tyrants do defeat.
Nor stony tower, nor walks of beaten brass,
Nor airless dungeon, nor strong links of iron,
Can be retentive to the strength of spirit;
But life, being weary of these worldly bars,
100 Never lacks power to dismiss itself.
If I know this, know all the world besides,
That part of tyranny that I do bear
I can shake off at pleasure.

Thunder still.

CASCA

So can I.
105 So every bondman in his own hand bears
The power to cancel his captivity.

CASSIUS

And why should Caesar be a tyrant then?
Poor man, I know he would not be a wolf
But that he sees the Romans are but sheep;
110 He were no lion, were not Romans hinds.
Those that with haste will make a mighty fire
Begin it with weak straws. What trash is Rome,
What rubbish, and what offal, when it serves
For the base matter to illuminate
115 So vile a thing as Caesar! But, O grief,
Where hast thou led me? I, perhaps, speak this
Before a willing bondman; then, I know
My answer must be made. But I am armed,
And dangers are to me indifferent.

CASCA

Indeed, they say that the Senators plan
to make Caesar a king tomorrow,
and he will wear his crown by sea and land—   90
in every place except here in Italy.

CASSIUS

I know where I will wear this dagger then;
Cassius will free Cassius from slavery by suicide.
And, you gods, by making such an act possible, you make the
weak very strong;
and, you gods, by making such an act possible, you defeat
tyrants.   95
No stony tower, no walls of beaten brass,
no airless dungeon, no chains of strong iron
can imprison a mighty spirit;
for life, when it grows weary of worldly limitations,
always has the power to end itself.   100
If I know this, then let the rest of the world know it, too—
whatever form of tyranny I suffer,
I can shake it off whenever I please—that is, by killing myself.

The thunder continues.

CASCA

So can I.
For every slave holds in his own hand   105
the power to end his captivity.

CASSIUS

Why should Caesar be a tyrant, then?
Poor man, I know that he wouldn't be a wolf
if he didn't see that Romans are no more than sheep.
He wouldn't be a lion if he didn't see that Romans are deer.   110
Anyone who wants to make a mighty fire in a hurry
starts it with little straws. What kind of brush is Rome,
what kind of litter or wood chips, that it should be used
for kindling to light up
a worthless thing like Caesar? But—oh, grief,   115
what have you made me say? Perhaps I'm saying all this
to a willing slave; if so, I know
that I must answer for what I've said. But I am armed,
and dangers are unimportant to me.

CASCA

120 You speak to Casca, and to such a man
That is no fleering telltale. Hold. My hand.
Be factious for **redress** of all these griefs,
And I will set this foot of mine as far
As who goes farthest.

CASSIUS

125   There's a bargain made.
Now know you, Casca, I have moved already
Some certain of the noblest-minded Romans
To undergo with me an enterprise
Of honorable-dangerous consequence.
130 And I do know, by this they stay for me
In Pompey's Porch.* For now, this fearful night,
There is no stir or walking in the streets;
And the complexion of the element
In favor's like the work we have in hand,
135 Most bloody, fiery, and most terrible.

       Enter CINNA.

CASCA

Stand close awhile, for here comes one in haste.

CASSIUS

'Tis Cinna; I do know him by his gait.
He is a friend.—Cinna, where haste you so?

CINNA

To find out you. Who's that, Metellus Cimber?

CASSIUS

140 No, it is Casca, one incorporate
To our attempts. Am I not stayed for, Cinna?

CINNA

I am glad on 't. What a fearful night is this!
There's two or three of us have seen strange sights.

---

131   *Pompey's Porch* the portico or colonnade of the theater built by Pompey in the
Campus Martius in 55 B.C. Caesar's murder, which in Plutarch takes place in
Pompey's Porch, is transferred by Shakespeare to the Capitol, by which he means
the Senate House, a building also erected by Pompey.

CASCA

You're talking to Casca—and to a man 120
who is no sneering informer. Here, take my hand.
If you'll be active in the faction to set these grievances right,
I will go as far to help you
as anyone else does.

They shake hands.

CASSIUS

It's a deal, then. 125
Casca, you know that I've already persuaded
a few of the noblest-minded Romans
to undertake an enterprise with me
that will lead to honorable but dangerous results.
And I know that they're waiting for me right now 130
in Pompey's Porch. On this frightening night,
no one stirs or walks in the streets,
and the appearance of the sky
strongly resembles the work that we must do—
so bloody, fiery, and terrible. 135

CINNA enters.

CASCA

Keep hidden a moment, for here comes someone in a hurry.

CASSIUS

It's Cinna; I recognize him by his walk.
He is a friend.—Cinna, where are you off to in such a hurry?

CINNA.

Looking for you. Who's that? Metellus Cimber?

CASSIUS

No, it is Casca—someone closely united 140
with our cause. Aren't they waiting for me, Cinna?

CINNA.

I'm glad Casca's on our side. What a fearful night this is!
Two or three of us have seen some strange sights.

CASSIUS
Am I not stayed for? Tell me.

CINNA
145 Yes, you are. O Cassius, if you could
but win the noble Brutus to our party—

CASSIUS
Be you content. Good Cinna, take this paper,
And look you lay it in the Praetor's chair,
Where Brutus may but find it; and throw this
150 In at his window; set this up with wax
Upon old Brutus's* statue. All this done,
Repair to Pompey's Porch, where you shall find us.
Is Decius Brutus and Trebonius there?

CINNA
All but Metellus Cimber, and he's gone
155 To seek you at your house. Well, I will hie,
And so bestow these papers as you bade me.

CASSIUS
That done, repair to Pompey's Theater.

Exit CINNA.

Come, Casca, you and I will yet, ere day,
See Brutus at his house. Three parts of him
160 Is ours already, and the man entire
Upon the next encounter yields him ours.

CASCA
O, he sits high in all the people's hearts,
And that which would appear offense in us,
His countenance, like richest alchemy,
165 Will change to virtue and to worthiness.

CASSIUS
Him and his worth and our great need of him
You have right well conceited. Let us go,
For it is after midnight, and ere day
We will awake him and be sure of him.

Exeunt.

---

151   *old Brutus's* Lucius Junius Brutus (the earlier Brutus who established the Roman Republic)

CASSIUS

Aren't they waiting for me? Tell me.

CINNA.

Yes, they are. Oh, Cassius, if you can   145
only persuade the noble Brutus to join our faction—

CASSIUS

Don't worry. Good Cinna, take this letter,
and be sure to lay it on the chief magistrate's chair,
where only Brutus can find it; and throw this one
into his window; and fasten this one with wax   150
to old Brutus's statue. Once you've done this,
return to Pompey's Porch, where you will find us.
Are Decius Brutus and Trebonius there?

CINNA

Everyone except Metellus Cimber, who went
to look for you at your house. Well, I will hurry   155
and put these papers where you told me to.

CASSIUS

When you've done that, return to Pompey's Theater.

> CINNA *exits.*

Come along, Casca. Before daybreak, you and I
will visit Brutus at his house. He is three-quarters
on our side already, and when we next meet him,   160
the entire man will join our faction.

CASCA

Oh, all the people think highly of him in their hearts;
and deeds which would seem wicked on our part,
his approval will transform till they appear
virtuous and worthy—as if by the most wonderful alchemy.   165

CASSIUS

You have correctly described Brutus, his value,
and our great need of him. Let's go,
for it is after midnight, and before daybreak,
we will awaken him and make sure he's on our side.

> *They exit.*

Act I Review

Discussion Questions

1. What do you think is the purpose of the quarrel between the senators and the commoners at the beginning of the play?

2. Caesar is suspicious of Cassius. Identify four qualities in Cassius that Caesar does not like.

3. How do we learn what kind of relationship Caesar and Brutus have had?

4. Read Cassius's description of Caesar in Scene ii. What does it tell you about his character as well as Caesar's character?

5. In Scene ii, Casca says that after being offered the crown, Caesar fainted and fell down on the ground. Do you think that Caesar really fainted? Explain why or why not.

6. What is revealed in Cassius's rebuke to Casca during the storm?

Literary Elements

1. A **pun** is a play on a word that may have one sound but more than one possible spelling or meaning. Find a pun in Act I, and explain its different meanings. Why do you think Shakespeare used the pun here?

2. **Foreshadowing** means clues or suggestions about later events in a plot. What examples of foreshadowing do you find in Act I?

3. A **simile** is a comparison of two unlike things using *like* or *as*. Find a simile in this act. How does it strengthen the description of the person, place, or thing being compared?

4. **Conflict** refers to struggle between opposing forces. Identify the different opinions that people—Brutus, Cassius, Casca, and the commoners—have about Caesar's character and role as a Roman ruler in Act I. Because of these differences, what conflicts are brewing?

Writing Prompts

1. Write a description of Brutus, Cassius, or Julius Caesar based on what you have learned about that man so far. Use specific quotes from the play to support your writing.

2. Write a newspaper account of Caesar's refusal of the crown of Rome on the day of the Lupercal festivities. Make sure to interview at least three or four bystanders. Remember, newsreaders expect answers to the questions who, what, where, when, and, if possible, why or how.

3. Look up the word *conspiracy* in the dictionary. Are there ever any good reasons for conspiring to overthrow a ruler or government? Now decide if there are any good reasons for the conspiracy against Caesar. Back up your opinions with examples.

4. Even today, some people believe in superstitions about the weather or animals. For example, you may have heard the saying "Red sky at morning, sailor take warning." Or you may know the belief that if a groundhog sees its shadow on February 2, there will be six more weeks of winter. List five or six of these superstitions, and then make up one of your own. Explain why your superstition might seem believable.

5. In Shakespeare's time, Elizabethan schoolchildren kept track of expressions known as "commonplaces"—catchphrases that seemed to contain some truth. *Julius Caesar*, like all of Shakespeare's plays, is filled with such pithy phrases, for example: "Cowards die many times before their deaths." Begin your own book of commonplaces by filling it with lines from the play that you find especially true or memorable.

JULIUS CAESAR

ACT II

Jason Robards, as Brutus, and Diana Rigg, as Portia, Peter Snells director, 1970

"DWELL I BUT IN THE SUBURBS
OF YOUR GOOD PLEASURE?"

Before You Read

1. How do you feel about Cassius at this point in the play? Think about what he might be up to and why.

2. What do you think of Brutus at this point? Discuss how he might respond to Cassius's plans and deceptions.

3. Have you ever trusted someone and then found out that you were mistaken? Consider how you would feel if a close friend turned against you.

4. If you were warned repeatedly that someone's dreams or visions foretold danger to you, how would you respond? Think about how Caesar might respond.

Literary Elements

1. A **soliloquy** is a speech that reveals the innermost thoughts and feelings of the character who speaks it. The speech is for the benefit of the audience, not the other characters. The most famous example from Shakespeare is the "to be or not to be" soliloquy by the title character in *Hamlet*.

2. **Irony** refers to the distance between appearance and reality. In Act I, it is ironic when the crowd cheers Caesar for turning down the crown because he is power hungry and trying not to show it.

3. A character's **motivation** is the combination of forces that make that person act as he or she does. In Act I, we learn that Casca and Cassius are both motivated to convert Brutus to their point of view so that he will help them get rid of Caesar.

4. A **theme** is a major idea or message of a play. One of the major themes of *Julius Caesar* is the effect of power on rulers and those whom they rule.

Words to Know

The following vocabulary words appear in Act II in the original text of Shakespeare's play. However, they are words that are still commonly used. Read the definitions here and pay attention to the words as you read the play (they will be in boldfaced type).

affability	friendliness; amiability
augmented	increased; intensified
augurers	those who predict
chide	scold; punish
dank	disagreeably moist
gravity	seriousness; importance
imminent	about to happen; coming up
instigations	things begun or started
insurrection	rebellion; mutiny
prevail	succeed; triumph
prodigies	extraordinary or meaningful events

Act Summary

Shortly before daybreak on March 15, Brutus is walking alone in his orchard. For weeks he has been unable to sleep because he has been debating what to do about Caesar. Finally he decides that Caesar's grab for power must be stopped and Rome saved from Caesar's tyranny.

Cassius and the other conspirators visit Brutus in the night and learn that he is going to join them. A man of principles, Brutus makes it clear that the men must act in ways that make them appear noble and not ambitious or jealous of Caesar. In his heart, he believes that assassinating Caesar is necessary to protect Roman liberties and prevent the abuses of monarchy. After the conspirators leave, Brutus's wife, Portia, pleads with him to share what is troubling him. When he refuses, she shows him a wound she has inflicted upon her thigh to prove her love for him.

At home, Caesar is unsure whether to go to the Capitol on the day the Soothsayer warned him about, the ides of March. His superstitions are fed by his wife Calphurnia's dream that he will be murdered. Decius, one of the conspirators, arrives and persuades Caesar to go, appealing to his ambition and vanity. Ultimately Caesar decides that he cannot appear to be afraid. And so he makes plans to attend with his "friends," the plotters who have gathered at his home.

In the street waiting for Caesar to appear, Artemidorus reads a letter he plans to give Caesar that will reveal the plot against his life. At home after Brutus has left for the Capitol, Portia is frantic with worry. Knowing the conspirators' plan, she anxiously awaits word of events at the Capitol.

ACT II, SCENE I

[Rome.] Enter BRUTUS *in his orchard.*

BRUTUS
What, Lucius, ho!—
I cannot, by the progress of the stars,
Give guess how near to day.—Lucius, I say!—
I would it were my fault to sleep so soundly.—
5   When, Lucius, when? Awake, I say! What, Lucius!

Enter LUCIUS.

LUCIUS
Called you, my lord?

BRUTUS
Get me a taper in my study, Lucius;
When it is lighted, come and call me here.

LUCIUS
I will, my lord.

Exit.

BRUTUS
10   It must be by his death. And for my part,
I know no personal cause to spurn at him,
But for the general: he would be crowned.
How that might change his nature, there's the question.
It is the bright day that brings forth the adder,
15   And that craves wary walking. Crown him that
And then I grant we put a sting in him,
That at his will he may do danger with.
Th' abuse of greatness is when it disjoins
Remorse from power. And to speak truth of Caesar,
20   I have not known when his affections swayed
More than his reason. But 'tis a common proof
That lowliness is young ambition's ladder,
Whereto the climber upward turns his face;

ACT 2, SCENE 1

Rome. Brutus's garden. BRUTUS *enters.*

BRUTUS
Lucius, come here!
By the movements of the stars, I can't
guess how close it is to day. Lucius, I called you!
I wish it were a fault of mine to sleep so soundly.
When are you coming, Lucius? Wake up, I tell you! Come   5
    on, Lucius!

    LUCIUS *enters.*

LUCIUS
Did you call, my lord?

BRUTUS
Put a candle in my study, Lucius.
Once you've lighted it, come back here to me.

LUCIUS
I will, my lord.

    Exits.

BRUTUS
Caesar's death is the only way. But for my part,   10
I don't know any personal reason to rebel against him—
only the public welfare. He wishes to be crowned.
How that might change his character—that's the problem.
The viper comes out in broad daylight,
so that's when one must walk with care. If we crown him
    as king,   15
I must admit, we'll give him an ability to bite
that he can use to do harm at will.
Greatness is most abused when mercy
becomes disconnected from power. To be honest about Caesar,
I've never known him to let his emotions   20
get the better of his judgment. But it's commonly seen
that humility is a ladder for budding ambition,
for the climber must keep his face turned upward;

But when he once attains the upmost round,
25 He then unto the ladder turns his back,
Looks in the clouds, scorning the base degrees*
By which he did ascend. So Caesar may;
Then lest he may, prevent. And since the quarrel
Will bear no color for the thing he is,
30 Fashion it thus: that what he is, **augmented**,
Would run to these and these extremities.
And therefore think him as a serpent's egg,
Which hatched, would as his kind grow mischievous,
And kill him in the shell.

Enter LUCIUS.

LUCIUS
35 The taper burneth in your closet, sir.
Searching the window for a flint, I found
This paper, thus sealed up, and I am sure
It did not lie there when I went to bed.

Gives him the letter.

BRUTUS
Get you to bed again. It is not day.
40 Is not tomorrow, boy, the ides of March?

LUCIUS
I know not, sir.

BRUTUS
Look in the calendar and bring me word.

LUCIUS
I will, sir.

Exit.

BRUTUS
The exhalations, whizzing in the air,
45 Gives so much light that I may read by them.

---

26 *base degrees* Brutus is thinking about the lower public offices from which Caesar
has risen, and the base and vile public by whose favor he has been able to attain
"the upmost round."

but once he has reached the topmost rung,
he turns his back on the ladder   25
and looks into the clouds and scoffs at the lowly rungs
by which he climbed. Caesar might do so as well;
and since he might, we should take action to forestall him. And
    since our accusation
cannot be justified according to what Caesar is right now,
let's argue the case this way: if his personality becomes   30
    exaggerated,
it will tend toward such and such extremes;
and therefore, let's think of him as a serpent in its egg—
once it is hatched, it will grow harmful by its very nature;
so let's kill Caesar in his shell.

       LUCIUS enters.

LUCIUS
The candle is burning in your study, sir.   35
When I was looking for a flint near the window, I found
this sealed letter, and I am sure
it wasn't lying there when I went to bed.

       LUCIUS gives him the letter.

BRUTUS
Go back to bed; it's not yet day.
Isn't tomorrow March 15, boy?   40

LUCIUS
I don't know, sir.

BRUTUS
Check the calendar and tell me.

LUCIUS
I will, sir.

       Exit.

BRUTUS
These meteors whizzing through the air
give so much light, I can read this letter by them.   45

Opens the letter and reads.

"Brutus, thou sleep'st. Awake, and see thyself!
Shall Rome, &c. Speak, strike, redress!"
"Brutus, thou sleep'st. Awake!"
Such **instigations** have been often dropped
50 Where I have took them up.
"Shall Rome, &c." Thus must I piece it out:
Shall Rome stand under one man's awe? What, Rome?
My ancestors did from the streets of Rome
The Tarquin drive when he was called a king.
55 "Speak, strike, redress!" Am I entreated
To speak and strike? O Rome, I make thee promise,
If the redress will follow, thou receivest
Thy full petition at the hand of Brutus.

Enter LUCIUS.

LUCIUS
Sir, March is wasted fifteen days.

Knock within.

BRUTUS
60 'Tis good. Go to the gate; somebody knocks.

[*Exit* LUCIUS.]

Since Cassius first did whet me against Caesar,
I have not slept.
Between the acting of a dreadful thing
And the first motion, all the interim is
65 Like a phantasma or a hideous dream.
The Genius* and the mortal instruments
Are then in council, and the state of a man,
Like to a little kingdom, suffers then
The nature of an **insurrection**.

Enter LUCIUS.

LUCIUS
70 Sir, 'tis your brother* Cassius at the door,
Who doth desire to see you.

---

66 *Genius* The Romans believed that each man had a guardian spirit that attended
him from birth (the same as the Greek "daemon" or "demon").

70 *brother* brother-in-law. Cassius was married to Junia, the sister of Brutus.

He opens the letter and reads it.

Brutus, you are asleep; wake up and look at yourself.
must Rome, et cetera. Speak, strike, set things right!
"Brutus, you are asleep. Wake up!"
Provocative letters like these have often been dropped
where I could pick them up.   50
"Must Rome, et cetera." Here's how I must fill in the meaning:
Must Rome stand in awe of one man? What—Rome?
My ancestors drove Tarquin
from the streets of Rome when he was a king.
"Speak, strike, set things right!" Am I being asked   55
to speak and strike? Oh, Rome, I make you this promise:
if it will set things right, you will receive
all that you ask for from Brutus's hands.

    LUCIUS enters.

LUCIUS

Sir, fifteen days have already passed in March.

    Knocking offstage.

BRUTUS

That's good. Go to the gate; somebody is knocking.   60

    LUCIUS exits.

Ever since Cassius first incited me against Caesar,
I haven't slept.
Between the first proposal of a dreadful thing
and the actual doing of it, everything in between is
like an hallucination or a frightful dream.   65
A man's guiding spirit and the limbs of his body
become locked in a fierce debate; and then the individual,
like a little kingdom, suffers from
a sort of rebellion.

    LUCIUS enters.

LUCIUS

Sir, your brother-in-law Cassius is at the door   70
and wants to see you.

BRUTUS

                       Is he alone?

LUCIUS

  No, sir, there are more with him.

BRUTUS

                    Do you know them?

LUCIUS

75 No, sir; their hats are plucked about their ears,
  And half their faces buried in the cloaks,
  That by no means I may discover them
  By any mark of favor.

BRUTUS

               Let 'em enter.

    [*Exit* LUCIUS.]

80 They are the faction. O conspiracy,
  Sham'st thou to show thy dang'rous brow by night,
  When evils are most free? O then, by day
  Where wilt thou find a cavern dark enough
  To mask thy monstrous visage? Seek none, conspiracy;
85 Hide it in smiles and **affability**.
  For if thou path, thy native semblance on,
  Not Erebus itself were dim enough
  To hide thee from prevention.

      Enter the conspirators, CASSIUS, CASCA, DECIUS,
      CINNA, METELLUS, *and* TREBONIUS.

CASSIUS

  I think we are too bold upon your rest.
90 Good morrow, Brutus. Do we trouble you?

BRUTUS

  I have been up this hour, awake all night.
  Know I these men that come along with you?

CASSIUS

  Yes, every man of them; and no man here
  But honors you, and every one doth wish
95 You had but that opinion of yourself

BRUTUS
Is he alone?

LUCIUS
No, sir—there are others with him.

BRUTUS
Do you know them?

LUCIUS
No, sir. Their hats are pulled down around their ears,　　75
and their faces are half covered by their cloaks,
so there is no way for me to recognize them
by any of their features.

BRUTUS
Let them come in.

　　LUCIUS *exits.*

It is the faction that opposes Caesar. Oh, conspiracy,　　80
are you ashamed to show your dangerous face even by night,
when evils are most free? Well then, by day,
where will you find a cavern dark enough
to hide your monstrous appearance? Don't look for a cavern,
　　conspiracy.
Hide yourself in smiles and pleasantness,　　85
for if you go walking undisguised,
not even Erebus is dark enough
to hide you from being stopped.

　　The conspirators—CASSIUS, CASCA, DECIUS, CINNA,
　　METELLUS, *and* TREBONIUS—*enter.*

CASSIUS
I'm afraid we've been too bold in disturbing your sleep.
Good morning, Brutus. Are we disturbing you?　　90

BRUTUS
I'm up at this hour because I've been awake all night.
Do I know these men who have come along with you?

CASSIUS
Yes, every one of them. And there's not a man here
who doesn't respect you, and every one wishes
that you held the same high opinion of yourself　　95

Which every noble Roman bears of you.
This is Trebonius.

BRUTUS

He is welcome hither.

CASSIUS

This, Decius Brutus.

BRUTUS

100   He is welcome too.

CASSIUS

This, Casca; this, Cinna; and this, Metellus Cimber.

BRUTUS

They are all welcome.
What watchful cares do interpose themselves
Betwixt your eyes and night?

CASSIUS

105   Shall I entreat a word?

They whisper.

DECIUS

Here lies the east. Doth not the day break here?

CASCA

No.

CINNA

O pardon, sir, it doth; and yon gray lines
That fret the clouds are messengers of day.

CASCA

110   You shall confess that you are both deceived.
Here, as I point my sword, the sun arises,
Which is a great way growing on the south,
Weighing the youthful season of the year.
Some two months hence, up higher toward the north
115   He first presents his fire; and the high east
Stands, as the Capitol, directly here.

BRUTUS [*coming forward with* CASSIUS]
Give me your hands all over, one by one.

that all noble Romans hold of you.
This is Trebonius.

BRUTUS
He is welcome here.

CASSIUS
This is Decius Brutus.

BRUTUS
He is welcome too.   100

CASSIUS
This is Casca; this is Cinna; and this is Metellus Cimber.

BRUTUS
They are all welcome.
What worries are keeping you awake, putting themselves
between your eyes and night?

CASSIUS
May I have a word with you?   105

> BRUTUS *and* CASSIUS *whisper to each other.*

DECIUS
That way is east. Isn't the day breaking there?

CASCA
No.

CINNA
Oh, pardon me, sir, but it is; and those gray lines
interlacing the clouds are like messengers announcing daylight.

CASCA
You will have to admit that you are both incorrect.   110
There, where I'm pointing my sword, is where the sun rises;
it is moving quite far toward the south,
considering how early it is in the year.
Some two months from now, the sun will first appear
farther toward the north; and due east   115
is directly over there, where the Capitol is.

BRUTUS [*coming forward with* CASSIUS]
All of you give me your hands, one by one.

CASSIUS

And let us swear our resolution.

BRUTUS

No, not an oath. If not the face of men,
120 The sufferance of our souls, the time's abuse—
If these be motives weak, break off betimes,
And every man hence to his idle bed.
So let high-sighted tyranny range on
Till each man drop by lottery. But if these,
125 As I am sure they do, bear fire enough
To kindle cowards and to steel with valor
The melting spirits of women, then, countrymen,
What need we any spur but our own cause
To prick us to redress? What other bond
130 Than secret Romans that have spoke the word
And will not palter? And what other oath
Than honesty to honesty engaged
That this shall be or we will fall for it?
Swear priests and cowards and men cautelous,
135 Old feeble carrions and such suffering souls
That welcome wrongs. Unto bad causes swear
Such creatures as men doubt; but do not stain
The even virtue of our enterprise,
Nor th' insuppressive mettle of our spirits,
140 To think that or our cause or our performance
Did need an oath; when every drop of blood
That every Roman bears, and nobly bears,
Is guilty of a several bastardy
If he do break the smallest particle
145 Of any promise that hath passed from him.

CASSIUS

But what of Cicero? Shall we sound him?
I think he will stand very strong with us.

CASCA

Let us not leave him out.

CASSIUS

And let us swear an oath to our decision.

BRUTUS

No, not an oath. Consider the faces of our fellow citizens,
the distress of our own souls, the corruption of our age.   120
If these are weak motives, let's stop what we're doing
    immediately,
and let every man go back to his comfortable bed.
And so let the arrogant tyrant continue on his course
until every man dies at his whim. But if our motives
are urgent enough (as I'm sure they are)   125
to fire up cowards and to harden the melting
spirits of women with courage—then, countrymen,
why do we need any spur but our own cause
to incite us to find a remedy? What more do we need to commit
    ourselves,
than the fact that we are discreet Romans who promise to
    do a thing   130
and will not waver? And what oath do we need,
other than to honorably promise one another
that we'll succeed, or die in the attempt?
Oaths are for priests, cowards, overly cautious men,
half-dead wretches, and long-suffering souls   135
who are looking for trouble; creatures that men distrust
swear oaths for their bad causes. So let's not stain
the straightforward justice of our undertaking,
or the irrepressible character of our spirits,
by thinking that either our cause or its outcome   140
needs an oath; for every drop of blood
that every Roman holds—and holds nobly—
betrays itself as shamefully un-Roman
if he breaks even the smallest part
of any promise he has made.   145

CASSIUS

But what about Cicero? Should we find out what he thinks about
    this?
I think he would stand very strongly with us.

CASCA

Let's not leave him out.

CINNA

No, by no means.

METELLUS

150 O let us have him, for his silver hairs*
Will purchase us a good opinion
And buy men's voices to commend our deeds.
It shall be said his judgment ruled our hands.
Our youths and wildness shall no whit appear,
155 But all be buried in his **gravity**.

BRUTUS

O name him not! Let us not break with him,
For he will never follow anything
That other men begin.

CASSIUS

Then leave him out.

CASCA

160 Indeed, he is not fit.

DECIUS

Shall no man else be touched, but only Caesar?

CASSIUS

Decius, well urged. I think it is not meet
Mark Antony, so well beloved of Caesar,
Should outlive Caesar. We shall find of him
165 A shrewd contriver. And, you know, his means,
If he improve them, may well stretch so far
As to annoy us all; which to prevent,
Let Antony and Caesar fall together.

BRUTUS

Our course will seem too bloody, Caius Cassius,
170 To cut the head off and then hack the limbs
Like wrath in death and envy afterwards;
For Antony is but a limb of Caesar.
Let's be sacrificers, but not butchers, Caius.

---

150 *silver hairs* a reference both to Cicero's age and to his reputation for dignity
(from the purity and brightness of silver). Metellus is also thinking of silver as a
word for money (note "purchase" and "buy" in the next lines), perhaps as the
price of betrayal (as Judas betrayed Christ for thirty pieces of silver).

CINNA

No, by no means.

METELLUS

Oh, let us include him, for his silver hair   150
will bring us a better reputation,
and cause men's voices to praise our deeds.
It will be said that his judgment ruled our hands.
No one will blame what we do on youth and wildness,
for his dignity will reflect well on us.   155

BRUTUS

Oh, don't bring him into it! Let's not tell him our plans,
for he will never go along with anything
that other men begin.

CASSIUS

Then leave him out.

CASCA

Indeed, he's not right for us.   160

DECIUS

Should we do away with anyone besides Caesar?

CASSIUS

That's well suggested, Decius. I don't think it's proper
for Mark Antony to outlive Caesar,
since he's so loved by Caesar. We will find that he's
a cunning plotter. And you know that if   165
he makes good use of his resources, he might succeed
in harming us all. To forestall this,
let Antony and Caesar die together.

BRUTUS

Our deed will seem too bloody, Caius Cassius—
to cut off the head and then hack off the limbs,   170
as if we killed Caesar out of anger, then showed hatred
    afterwards,
because Antony is only a limb of Caesar.
Let's be sacrificers, but not butchers, Caius.

We all stand up against the spirit of Caesar,
175 And in the spirit of men there is no blood.
O that we then could come by Caesar's spirit
And not dismember Caesar! But, alas,
Caesar must bleed for it. And, gentle* friends,
Let's kill him boldly, but not wrathfully.
180 Let's carve him as a dish fit for the gods,
Not hew him as a carcass fit for hounds.
And let our hearts, as subtle masters do,
Stir up their servants to an act of rage,
And after seem to **chide** 'em. This shall make
185 Our purpose necessary, and not envious;
Which so appearing to the common eyes,
We shall be called purgers, not murderers.
And for Mark Antony, think not of him,
For he can do no more than Caesar's arm
190 When Caesar's head is off.

CASSIUS
                    Yet I fear him,
For in the ingrafted love he bears to Caesar—

BRUTUS
Alas, good Cassius, do not think of him.
If he love Caesar, all that he can do
195 Is to himself: take thought and die for Caesar.
And that were much he should, for he is given
To sports, to wildness, and much company.

TREBONIUS
There is no fear in him. Let him not die,
For he will live and laugh at this hereafter.

Clock strikes.

BRUTUS
200 Peace! Count the clock.

CASSIUS
                    The clock hath stricken three.

---

178 *gentle* wordplay in two senses: having the quality of a gentleman and not being
harsh or violent. It is a typical irony of Brutus that he should call his friends
"gentle" in the very sentence that he is asking them to kill Caesar.

We are fighting against the tyrannical spirit of Caesar—
and in men's spirits, there is no blood.   175
Oh, if only we could get at Caesar's spirit
and not dismember Caesar! But alas,
Caesar must shed blood because of his spirit. And, noble friends,
let's kill him boldly, but without anger.
Let's carve him as if he were a dish fit for the gods,   180
not hack him up like a carcass fit for hounds.
And let our hearts be like cunning masters,
and stir up their servants—our hands—to an act of rage,
then afterwards seem to scold them for it. This will show
that we acted out of necessity, not hatred;   185
and because it will appear so in the commoners' eyes,
we will be called healers, not murderers.
As for Mark Antony, don't worry about him—
for he won't be able to do more than Caesar's arm could do
if Caesar's head were cut off.   190

CASSIUS

Still, I'm afraid of him
because of the deep-rooted love he has for Caesar—

BRUTUS

Alas, good Cassius, don't worry about him.
If he loves Caesar, the only thing he'll be able to do
is to himself: grieve for Caesar, then commit suicide.   195
And that's too much to expect of him, because he's devoted
to sports, wild partying, and his many friends.

TREBONIUS

There's nothing to fear from him. He doesn't need to die.
For if he lives, he'll laugh it off eventually.

A clock strikes.

BRUTUS

Quiet! Count the strokes of the clock.   200

CASSIUS

The clock has struck three.

TREBONIUS

'Tis time to part.

CASSIUS

But it is doubtful yet
Whether Caesar will come forth today or no,
205 For he is superstitious grown of late,
Quite from the main opinion he held once
Of fantasy, of dreams, and ceremonies.
It may be these apparent **prodigies**,
The unaccustomed terror of this night,
210 And the persuasion of his **augurers**,
May hold him from the Capitol today.

DECIUS

Never fear that. If he be so resolved,
I can o'ersway him; for he loves to hear
That unicorns may be betrayed with trees,
215 And bears with glasses, elephants with holes,
Lions with toils and men with flatterers.
But when I tell him he hates flatterers,
He says he does, being then most flattered.
Let me work,
220 For I can give his humor the true bent,
And I will bring him to the Capitol.

CASSIUS

Nay, we will all of us be there to fetch him.

BRUTUS

By the eighth hour, is that the uttermost?

CINNA

Be that the uttermost, and fail not then.

METELLUS

225 Caius Ligarius doth bear Caesar hard,
Who rated him for speaking well of Pompey.
I wonder none of you have thought of him.

BRUTUS

No, good Metellus, go along by him.
He loves me well, and I have given him reasons.
230 Send him but hither, and I'll fashion him.

TREBONIUS
It's time to go.

CASSIUS
But it's still uncertain
whether Caesar will come out today or not,
for he has grown superstitious lately—   205
quite contrary to the great disdain he once had
for fantasies, dreams, and omens.
It could be that these clear signs of disaster,
the unusual terrors of this night,
and the influence of his priests   210
might keep him away from the Capitol today.

DECIUS
Don't worry about that. If he's decided to stay home,
I can talk him out of it—for he loves to be told
that unicorns can be impaled on trees,
bears caught with mirrors, elephants with pitfalls,   215
lions with nets, and men with flattery.
But when I tell him that he hates flatterers,
he always agrees with me—for that's very flattering to him.
Let me work on him,
for I can turn his mood in the right direction,   220
and I will bring him to the Capitol.

CASSIUS
No, all of us will go there to get him.

BRUTUS
By eight o'clock—isn't that the latest time to go?

CINNA
Let that be the latest; don't fail to be there by then.

METELLUS
Caius Ligarius has a grudge against Caesar,   225
who berated him for speaking well of Pompey.
I wonder why none of you thought about including him.

BRUTUS
Good Metellus, call on him at his house.
He loves me well, and I have given him reasons to join us.
Send him here, and I will talk him into joining us.   230

CASSIUS

The morning comes upon 's. We'll leave you, Brutus.
And, friends, disperse yourselves; but all remember
What you have said, and show yourselves true Romans.

BRUTUS

Good gentlemen, look fresh and merrily.
235 Let not our looks put on our purposes,
But bear it as our Roman actors do,
With untired spirits and formal constancy.
And so good morrow to you every one.

Exeunt. BRUTUS remains.

Boy! Lucius!—Fast asleep? It is no matter.
240 Enjoy the honey-heavy dew of slumber.
Thou hast no figures nor no fantasies
Which busy care draws in the brains of men.
Therefore thou sleep'st so sound.

Enter PORTIA.

PORTIA

                                   Brutus, my lord.

BRUTUS

245 Portia! What mean you? Wherefore rise you now?
It is not for your health thus to commit
Your weak condition to the raw cold morning.

PORTIA

Nor for yours neither. Y' have ungently, Brutus,
Stole from my bed. And yesternight at supper
250 You suddenly arose and walked about,
Musing and sighing, with your arms across;
And when I asked you what the matter was,
You stared upon me with ungentle looks.
I urged you further; then you scratched your head,
255 And too impatiently stamped with your foot.
Yet I insisted, yet you answered not,
But with an angry wafture of your hand
Gave sign for me to leave you. So I did,
Fearing to strengthen that impatience
260 Which seemed too much enkindled; and withal

CASSIUS

Morning has arrived. We'll leave you, Brutus.
And, friends, go your different ways; but all of you remember
what you have said, and prove yourselves to be true Romans.

BRUTUS

Good gentlemen, look rested and happy.
Don't let our expressions betray our plans,   235
but let's play our parts like our Roman actors do—
with tireless spirits and dignified calm.
And so, good day to every one of you.

> *Everyone but* BRUTUS *exits.*

Boy! Lucius!—Are you fast asleep? It doesn't matter.
Enjoy the heavy, honey-like refreshment of sleep.   240
You don't suffer from strange figments of imagination,
which busy worry draws in men's brains—
and that's why you sleep so soundly.

> PORTIA *enters.*

PORTIA

Brutus, my lord.

BRUTUS

Portia, what are you doing? Why are you awake now?   245
It's not healthy for you to expose
your weak constitution to the rough, cold morning.

PORTIA

It's not healthy for you, either. Brutus, you disrespectfully
crept out of my bed. And last night during supper,
you suddenly got up and walked around,   250
thinking and sighing, with your arms crossed;
and when I asked you what was the matter,
you stared at me with an unkind expression.
I asked you again; then you scratched your head
and stamped your foot impatiently.   255
I kept insisting, and you still didn't answer,
but made a sign for me to leave you
with an angry wave of your hand. I did so,
fearing to add to your impatience,
which seemed already too stirred up; and also,   260

Hoping it was but an effect of humor,
Which sometime hath his hour with every man.
It will not let you eat, nor talk, nor sleep;
And could it work so much upon your shape
265　　As it hath much prevailed on your condition,
I should not know you Brutus. Dear my lord,
Make me acquainted with your cause of grief.

BRUTUS
I am not well in health, and that is all.

PORTIA
Brutus is wise, and were he not in health,
270　　He would embrace the means to come by it.

BRUTUS
Why so I do. Good Portia, go to bed.

PORTIA
Is Brutus sick? And is it physical
To walk unbraced and suck up the humors
Of the **dank** morning? What, is Brutus sick?
275　　And will he steal out of the wholesome bed
To dare the vile contagion of the night,*
And tempt the rheumy and unpurged air
To add unto his sickness? No, my Brutus,
You have some sick offense within your mind,
280　　Which by the right and virtue of my place
I ought to know of. And upon my knees,
I charm you, by my once commended beauty,
By all your vows of love, and that great vow
Which did incorporate and make us one,
285　　That you unfold to me, your self, your half,
Why you are heavy—and what men tonight
Have had resort to you; for here have been
Some six or seven, who did hide their faces
Even from darkness.

276　*vile contagion of the night* capacity of the night air to infect. In Shakespeare's time
it was generally believed that the night air could cause disease.

I hoped it was the symptom of some passing mood—
the kind that overcomes all men from time to time.
But it won't let you eat, talk, or sleep,
and if it could affect your physical shape
the way it has taken control of your state of mind,   265
I wouldn't even recognize you as Brutus. My dear lord,
let me know the cause of your sorrow.

BRUTUS

I'm not in good health, and that is all.

PORTIA

Brutus is wise, and if he weren't in good health,
he'd do whatever was necessary to regain it.   270

BRUTUS

Why, I am doing so. Good Portia, go to bed.

PORTIA

Is Brutus sick? And is it healthy
to walk around with your shirt open, breathing in the mist
of the damp morning? What, is Brutus sick?
And yet he creeps out of his healthy bed   275
and dares to face the filthy diseases of the night,
tempting the damp, impure air
to add to his sickness? No, my Brutus—
you have some sickness that harms your mind,
and as your wife, I've got every right   280
to know about it.

She kneels.

And on my knees,
I implore you, by my once-praised beauty,
by all your vows of love, and by that great vow of marriage
that joined us together as one flesh,
to tell me—your other self, your other half—   285
why you are sad. And tell me, who were those men
who came to see you tonight? For six or seven
of them have been here, hiding their faces
even from darkness.

BRUTUS

290   Kneel not, gentle Portia.

    [He lifts her up.]

PORTIA

I should not need, if you were gentle Brutus.
Within the bond of marriage, tell me, Brutus,
Is it excepted I should know no secrets
That appertain to you? Am I your self
295   But, as it were, in sort of limitation?
To keep with you at meals, comfort your bed,
And talk to you sometimes? Dwell I but in the suburbs*
Of your good pleasure? If it be no more,
Portia is Brutus's harlot, not his wife.

BRUTUS

300   You are my true and honorable wife,
As dear to me as are the ruddy drops
That visit my sad heart.

PORTIA

If this were true, then should I know this secret.
I grant I am a woman; but withal
305   A woman that Lord Brutus took to wife.
I grant I am a woman; but withal
A woman well reputed, Cato's* daughter.
Think you I am no stronger than my sex,
Being so fathered and so husbanded?
310   Tell me your counsels, I will not disclose 'em.
I have made strong proof of my constancy,
Giving myself a voluntary wound
Here, in the thigh. Can I bear that with patience,
And not my husband's secrets?

BRUTUS

315   O ye gods!
Render me worthy of this noble wife.

    Knock.

---

297   *suburbs* The connotation is that of a red-light district, and "suburbs" leads
directly to "harlot" in line 299. The suburbs of Shakespeare's London, especially
those of Southwark (the theater district across the Thames River), were notorious
for houses of prostitution.

BRUTUS

Do not kneel, gentle Portia. 290

He lifts her up.

PORTIA

I wouldn't need to if you were my gentle Brutus.
Tell me, Brutus—according to our bond of marriage,
may I know all secrets except the ones
that pertain to you? Am I your other self,
but only, so to speak, in a limited way— 295
to give you company at meals, comfort you in bed,
and talk to you sometimes? Do I live only in the outskirts
of your affection? If that's the case,
Portia is Brutus's whore, not his wife.

BRUTUS

You are my true and honored wife, 300
as precious to me as the red blood
that passes through my sad heart.

PORTIA

If that's true, then I should know this secret.
I admit I am a woman—but even so,
a woman that Lord Brutus chose for a wife. 305
I admit I am a woman—but even so,
a well-respected woman, Cato's daughter.
Do you think I am no stronger than other women,
with such a father and such a husband?
Tell me your secrets; I won't give them away. 310
I have put my own resolution to the test
by wounding myself of my own free will,
right here, in my thigh. Can I suffer the pain of that quietly
and not keep my husband's secrets?

BRUTUS

Oh, you gods, 315
make me worthy of this noble wife!

Knocking.

---

307   *Cato's* Marcus Porcius Cato was known, like his great-grandfather, Cato the
Censor, for the strict moral integrity of his life. He was the uncle of Brutus as well
as his father-in-law.

Hark, hark, one knocks. Portia, go in awhile,
And by and by thy bosom shall partake
The secrets of my heart.
320   All my engagements I will construe to thee,
All the charactery of my sad brows.
Leave me with haste.

     Exit PORTIA.

               Lucius, who's that knocks?

     Enter LUCIUS *and* LIGARIUS.

LUCIUS
Here is a sick man that would speak with you.

BRUTUS
325   Caius Ligarius, that Metellus spake of.—
Boy, stand aside. [*Exit* LUCIUS.]
            Caius Ligarius, how?

LIGARIUS
Vouchsafe good morrow from a feeble tongue.

BRUTUS
O what a time have you chose out, brave Caius,
330   To wear a kerchief! Would you were not sick!

LIGARIUS
I am not sick, if Brutus have in hand
Any exploit worthy the name of honor.

BRUTUS
Such an exploit have I in hand, Ligarius,
Had you a healthful ear to hear of it.

LIGARIUS
335   By all the gods that Romans bow before,
I here discard my sickness.

     [*takes off his kerchief*]

               Soul of Rome,
Brave son, derived from honorable loins,
Thou like an exorcist hast conjured up
340   My mortified spirit. Now bid me run,

Listen, listen—someone knocks. Portia, go away awhile,
and soon my bosom will share
the secrets of my heart with you.
I'll fully explain to you all my commitments   320
and the meaning of my sad expression.
Leave me quickly.

> PORTIA *exits.*

Lucius, who is that knocking?

> LUCIUS *and* LIGARIUS *enter.*

LUCIUS
A sick man is here who wants to speak with you.

BRUTUS
It's Caius Ligarius, whom Metellus spoke of.—   325
Boy, leave us. (LUCIUS *exits.*) How are you, Caius Ligarius?

LIGARIUS
Please accept a morning's greeting from my weak tongue.

BRUTUS
Oh, noble Caius, what a time you have chosen
to wear a cloth around your head! I wish you weren't sick!   330

LIGARIUS
I am not sick if Brutus is planning
any deed worthy to be called honorable.

BRUTUS
I am planning such a deed, Ligarius;
if only you had a healthy ear to hear about it.

LIGARIUS
By all the gods that Romans bow down to,   335
I now throw aside my sickness.

> *He takes off his cloth.*

You soul of Rome,
you brave son descended from an honorable ancestor—
like some exorcist, you have awakened my deadened spirit
by your spell. Now simply command me,   340

And I will strive with things impossible,
Yea, get the better of them. What's to do?

BRUTUS

A piece of work that will make sick men whole.

LIGARIUS

But are not some whole that we must make sick?

BRUTUS

345   That must we also. What it is, my Caius,
I shall unfold to thee, as we are going
To whom it must be done.

LIGARIUS

                    Set on your foot,
And with a heart new-fired I follow you,
350   To do I know not what; but it sufficeth
That Brutus leads me on.

      Thunder.

BRUTUS

                    Follow me then.

      Exeunt.

and I shall attempt to do impossible things—
indeed, I shall succeed. What needs to be done?

BRUTUS
A deed that will make sick men healthy.

LIGARIUS
But aren't some men healthy whom we must make sick?

BRUTUS
We must do that, too. My friend Caius, I will tell you   345
what it is while we are walking to the home of the person
it must be done to.

LIGARIUS
Start walking,
and with a heart rekindled with courage, I'll follow you,
not knowing what I must do; it's enough   350
that Brutus leads me on.

     Thunder.

BRUTUS
Follow me, then.

     They exit.

ACT II, SCENE II

[*Rome. Caesar's house.*] *Thunder and lightning. Enter*
JULIUS CAESAR *in his nightgown.*

CAESAR

Nor heaven nor earth have been at peace tonight.
Thrice has Calphurnia in her sleep cried out,
"Help, ho! They murder Caesar!"—Who's within?

Enter a SERVANT.

SERVANT

My lord.

CAESAR

5   Go bid the priests do present sacrifice,*
And bring me their opinions of success.

SERVANT

I will, my lord.

Exit.

Enter CALPHURNIA.

CALPHURNIA

What mean you, Caesar? Think you to walk forth?
You shall not stir out of your house today.

CAESAR

10   Caesar shall forth; the things that threatened me
Ne'er looked but on my back. When they shall see
The face of Caesar, they are vanished.

CALPHURNIA

Caesar, I never stood on ceremonies,
Yet now they fright me. There is one within,
15   Besides the things that we have heard and seen,
Recounts most horrid sights seen by the watch.

---

5   *sacrifice* Roman priests sacrificed various animals and examined their inner
organs as a way of predicting the future. Many other forms of forecasting were
practiced such as studying the flight of birds.

ACT 2, SCENE 2

Caesar's house. Thunder and lightning. JULIUS CAESAR *enters in his dressing gown.*

CAESAR
Neither heaven nor earth have been at peace tonight:
Three times, Calphurnia cried out in her sleep,
"Help, help! They're murdering Caesar!"—Who's there?

A SERVANT *enters.*

SERVANT
My lord?

CAESAR
Go order the priests to make a sacrifice immediately,   5
and bring me their judgments concerning the future.

SERVANT
I will, my lord.

SERVANT *exits;* CALPHURNIA *enters.*

CALPHURNIA
What are you going to do, Caesar? Are you thinking about going
    out?
You will not set foot out of the house today.

CAESAR
Caesar shall go out. The only things that have ever   10
    threatened me
were looking at my back; whenever they see
Caesar's face, they vanish.

CALPHURNIA
Caesar, I have never paid attention to omens,
but now they frighten me. Aside from the things
that we have heard and seen, there is someone in the   15
    other room
who tells of the most horrid sights seen by the night
    watchman.

A lioness hath whelped in the streets,
And graves have yawned and yielded up their dead.
Fierce fiery warriors fight upon the clouds

20 In ranks and squadrons and right form of war,
Which drizzled blood upon the Capitol.
The noise of battle hurtled in the air,
Horses did neigh, and dying men did groan,
And ghosts did shriek and squeal about the streets.

25 O Caesar, these things are beyond all use,
And I do fear them.

CAESAR
What can be avoided
Whose end is purposed by the mighty gods?
Yet Caesar shall go forth, for these predictions

30 Are to the world in general as to Caesar.

CALPHURNIA
When beggars die, there are no comets seen;
The heavens themselves blaze forth the death of princes.

CAESAR
Cowards die many times before their deaths;
The valiant never taste of death but once.

35 Of all the wonders that I yet have heard,
It seems to me most strange that men should fear,
Seeing that death, a necessary end,
Will come when it will come.

Enter a SERVANT.

What say the augurers?

SERVANT
40 They would not have you to stir forth today.
Plucking the entrails of an offering forth,
They could not find a heart within the beast.

CAESAR
The gods do this in shame of cowardice.
Caesar should be a beast without a heart

45 If he should stay at home today for fear.
No, Caesar shall not. Danger knows full well

A female lion gave birth in the streets,
and graves have opened and set free their dead.
Fierce, fiery warriors fought on the tops of clouds
in ranks, squadrons, and regular formations of battle,   20
causing blood to drizzle on the Capitol.
Battle noises clashed in the air,
horses neighed, dying men groaned,
and ghosts shrieked and squealed through the streets.
Oh, Caesar! These things are beyond normal experience,   25
and I'm afraid of them.

CAESAR

How can something be avoided
when the mighty gods have planned it to the end?
Even so, Caesar shall go out; for these omens
apply to the world in general, not just to Caesar.   30

CALPHURNIA

Comets don't appear to announce the deaths of beggars;
the heavens themselves catch fire to announce the deaths of
    great leaders.

CAESAR

Cowards die many times before their deaths;
the brave only taste death once.
Of all the wonders that I've ever heard of,   35
the strangest seems to me that men should feel fear—
considering that death, a necessary end,
will come when it will come.

     The SERVANT *reenters.*

What do the fortune-tellers say?

SERVANT

They don't want you to go out today.   40
When they took the entrails out of the sacrificed animal,
they couldn't find a heart inside.

CAESAR

The gods have done this to show how shameful cowardice is:
Caesar would be no more than an animal without a heart
if he stayed home today out of fear.   45
No, Caesar won't do that. My brother Danger knows full well

That Caesar is more dangerous than he.
We are two lions littered in one day,
And I the elder and more terrible,
50 And Caesar shall go forth.

CALPHURNIA

Alas, my lord,
Your wisdom is consumed in confidence.
Do not go forth today. Call it my fear
That keeps you in the house, and not your own.
55 We'll send Mark Antony to the Senate House,
And he shall say you are not well today.
Let me upon my knee **prevail** in this.

CAESAR

Mark Antony shall say I am not well,
And for thy humor I will stay at home.

Enter DECIUS.

60 Here's Decius Brutus; he shall tell them so.

DECIUS

Caesar, all hail! Good morrow, worthy Caesar.
I come to fetch you to the Senate House.

CAESAR

And you are come in very happy time
To bear my greeting to the Senators
65 And tell them that I will not come today.
Cannot is false, and that I dare not, falser.
I will not come today. Tell them so, Decius.

CALPHURNIA

Say he is sick.

CAESAR

Shall Caesar send a lie?
70 Have I in conquest stretched mine arm so far,
To be afeared to tell graybeards the truth?
Decius, go tell them Caesar will not come.

DECIUS

Most mighty Caesar, let me know some cause,
Lest I be laughed at when I tell them so.

that Caesar is more dangerous than he is;
we are two lions littered on the same day,
but I am older and more terrible.
And Caesar will go out.   50

CALPHURNIA
Alas, my lord,
your wisdom has been destroyed by too much confidence.
Do not go out today. Tell everyone it is my fear
that keeps you in the house and not your own.
We'll send Mark Antony to the Senate House,   55
and he will say you are not well today.
Let me convince you to do this, on my knees.

CAESAR
Mark Antony will say I am not well—
and because of this whim of yours, I will stay at home.

        DECIUS *enters.*

Here's Decius Brutus; he will tell them so.   60

DECIUS
All hail, Caesar! Good morning, worthy Caesar.
I've come to escort you to the Senate House.

CAESAR
And you've come at a very good moment
to take my greetings to the Senators
and tell them that I will not come today.   65
To say I "cannot" come would be false—and that I "dare" not,
    even falser.
I will not come today. Tell them that, Decius.

CALPHURNIA
Say he is sick.

CAESAR
Shall Caesar send them a lie?
Have I stretched my arm so far in conquest,   70
only to be afraid to tell old men the truth?
Decius, go tell them that Caesar will not come.

DECIUS
Most mighty Caesar, let me know some reason
so I won't be laughed at when I tell them so.

CAESAR

75   The cause is in my will: I will not come.
That is enough to satisfy the Senate.
But for your private satisfaction,
Because I love you, I will let you know.
Calphurnia here, my wife, stays me at home.

80   She dreamt tonight she saw my statue,
Which, like a fountain with an hundred spouts
Did run pure blood; and many lusty Romans
Came smiling and did bathe their hands in it.
And these does she apply for warnings and portents

85   And evils **imminent**; and on her knee
Hath begged that I will stay at home today.

DECIUS

This dream is all amiss interpreted;
It was a vision fair and fortunate.
Your statue spouting blood in many pipes,

90   In which so many smiling Romans bathed,
Signifies that from you great Rome shall suck
Reviving blood, and that great men shall press
For tinctures, stains, relics, and cognizance.*
This by Calphurnia's dream is signified.

CAESAR

95   And this way have you well expounded it.

DECIUS

I have, when you have heard what I can say—
And know it now: the Senate have concluded
To give this day a crown to mighty Caesar.
If you shall send them word you will not come,

100   Their minds may change. Besides, it were a mock
Apt to be rendered, for someone to say,
"Break up the Senate till another time,
When Caesar's wife shall meet with better dreams."
If Caesar hide himself, shall they not whisper,

105   "Lo, Caesar is afraid"?

---

93   *tinctures . . . cognizance* In alchemy, "tinctures" are quintessences or elixirs, and
in heraldry, the materials used in preparing a coat of arms. "Stains" are heraldic
colors, very close in meaning to "tinctures." "Cognizance" means "an heraldic
device or emblem worn by a nobleman's followers."

CAESAR

The reason is that I will it. I will not come. 75
That is enough to satisfy the Senate.
But because I love you, I will tell you the reason,
just for your personal satisfaction.
Calphurnia—my wife, here—is keeping me at home.
She dreamed last night that she saw my statue 80
pouring out pure blood, like a fountain
with a hundred spouts. And many happy,
smiling Romans came and bathed their hands in it.
She considers all this a warning and omen
of some approaching evil, and she has begged 85
on her knees for me to stay home today.

DECIUS

This dream has been very wrongly interpreted.
It was a pleasant and promising vision.
Your statue, pouring blood from many spouts
in which many smiling Romans bathed, 90
means that great Rome will drink revitalizing blood
from you, and that great men will crowd around you
to receive from you saintly relics and other symbols of power.
This is what Calphurnia's dream really means.

CAESAR

You have explained it all very well. 95

DECIUS

Yes, I have—and when you hear what I have to say,
you will be sure of it: the senators have decided
to give mighty Caesar a crown today.
If you send word to them that you're not coming,
they might change their minds. Besides, someone 100
is likely to say as a joke,
"Let the Senate break up until another time,
when Caesar's wife has had better dreams."
If Caesar hides himself, aren't they likely to whisper,
"See—Caesar is afraid"? 105

Pardon me, Caesar, for my dear dear love
To your proceeding bids me tell you this;
And reason to my love is liable.

CAESAR
How foolish do your fears seem now, Calphurnia!
110 I am ashamed I did yield to them.
Give me my robe, for I will go.

Enter BRUTUS, LIGARIUS, METELLUS, CASCA,
TREBONIUS, CINNA, *and* PUBLIUS.

And look where Publius is come to fetch me.

PUBLIUS
Good morrow, Caesar.

CAESAR
Welcome, Publius.—
115 What, Brutus, are you stirred so early too?—
Good morrow, Casca.—Caius Ligarius,
Caesar was ne'er so much your enemy*
As that same ague which hath made you lean.—
What is 't a clock?

BRUTUS
120 Caesar, 'tis strucken eight.

CAESAR
I thank you for your pains and courtesy.

Enter ANTONY.

See, Antony, that revels long a-nights,
Is notwithstanding up.—Good morrow, Antony.

ANTONY
So to most noble Caesar.

CAESAR
125 Bid them prepare within.
I am to blame to be thus waited for.
Now Cinna.—Now Metellus.—What, Trebonius,
I have an hour's talk in store for you.

---

117 *enemy* Ligarius had supported Pompey against Caesar in the Civil War and had
recently been pardoned by Caesar and had his civil rights restored.

Pardon me, Caesar, for having said all this
out of deep concern for your advancement;
my love for you has gotten the better of my judgment.

CAESAR
How foolish your fears seem now, Calphurnia!
I am ashamed of having given in to them.   110
Bring me my robe, for I will go.

> BRUTUS, LIGARIUS, METELLUS, CASCA, TREBONIUS, CINNA,
> *and* PUBLIUS *enter.*

And look—Publius has come to escort me.

PUBLIUS
Good morning, Caesar.

CAESAR
Welcome, Publius.—
What, Brutus, are you also up so early?—   115
Good morning, Casca.—Caius Ligarius,
Caesar was never as much of an enemy to you
as that fever which has made you so thin.—
What time is it?

BRUTUS
Caesar, the clock has struck eight.   120

CAESAR
I thank you for your trouble and courtesy.

> ANTONY *enters.*

Look—Antony is up, even though he parties
late at night.—Good morning, Antony.

ANTONY
The same to most noble Caesar.

CAESAR
Let the servants get some wine ready.   125
I am at fault for having taken so long.

> SERVANT *exits.*

Hello, Cinna.—Hello, Metellus.—Trebonius,
I have an hour of talk in store for you.

Remember that you call on me today;
130   Be near me, that I may remember you.

TREBONIUS
Caesar, I will. [*aside*] And so near will I be
That your best friends shall wish I had been further.

CAESAR
Good friends, go in and taste some wine with me,
And we, like friends, will straightway go together.

BRUTUS
135   [*aside*] That every like is not the same,* O Caesar,
The heart of Brutus earns to think upon.

Exeunt.

---

135   *That . . . same* Brutus picks up Caesar's phrase "like friends" and plays on the distinction between "like" and "same," similarity and identity, appearance and reality. The aside is ironic since Brutus's understanding of "like" is not the "same" as Caesar's. In other words, all uses of the word "like" do not have the "same" meaning.

Don't forget to pay me a visit today;
stay close to me so that I don't forget you.   130

TREBONIUS

Caesar, I will. (*aside*) I will be so close to you
that your best friends will wish I had been farther away.

CAESAR

Good friends, join me in the other room for some wine—
and we, like friends, will leave together soon for the Senate.

BRUTUS

(*aside*) Oh, Caesar, Brutus's heart grieves to think   135
that to be like friends isn't the same as being friends.

> *They exit.*

ACT II, SCENE III

[*Rome, a street.*] *Enter* ARTEMIDORUS [*reading a paper*].

ARTEMIDORUS
"Caesar, beware of Brutus; take heed of Cassius; come not
near Casca; have an eye to Cinna; trust not Trebonius;
mark well Metellus Cimber; Decius Brutus loves thee not;
thou hast wronged Caius Ligarius. There is but one mind
5 in all these men, and it is bent against Caesar. If thou
beest not immortal, look about you. Security gives way to
conspiracy. The mighty gods defend thee!

Thy lover,
Artemidorus."

10 Here will I stand till Caesar pass along,
And as a suitor will I give him this.
My heart laments that virtue cannot live
Out of the teeth of emulation.
If thou read this, O Caesar, thou mayest live;
15 If not, the Fates* with traitors do contrive.

Exit.

---

15 *Fates* in Greek mythology, the three goddesses who ruled the lives and destinies
of men: Clotho, who spun the thread of life; Lachesis, who measured out its
length; and Atropos, who cut it off at death

ACT 2, SCENE 3

A street near the Capitol, near Brutus's house. ARTEMIDORUS *enters, reading a letter.*

ARTEMIDORUS

Caesar, beware of Brutus, be careful of Cassius, don't go near Casca,
keep an eye on Cinna, don't trust Trebonius, watch out
for Metellus Cimber. Decius Brutus does not love you. You
have wronged Caius Ligarius. These men all have only one purpose,
and it is set against Caesar. Unless you're immortal,   5
watch out. Your overconfidence will help the conspirators.
May the mighty gods defend you!

> *Your devoted friend,*
> *Artemidorus.*

I'll stand right here until Caesar passes by,   10
and I will give him this letter as if I were a petitioner.
My heart is sad that virtuous men can't live
out of the reach of envious rivalry.
Oh, Caesar—if you read this, you might live;
if not, the Fates are plotting together with the traitors.   15

He exits.

ACT II, SCENE IV

[*Rome, before the house of Brutus.*] *Enter* PORTIA *and* LUCIUS.

PORTIA
I prithee, boy, run to the Senate House.
Stay not to answer me, but get thee gone.
Why dost thou stay?

LUCIUS
To know my errand, madam.

PORTIA
5 I would have had thee there and here again
Ere I can tell thee what thou shouldst do there.
[*aside*] O constancy, be strong upon my side,
Set a huge mountain 'tween my heart and tongue.
I have a man's mind but a woman's might.
10 How hard it is for women to keep counsel!*
—Art thou here yet?

LUCIUS
Madam, what should I do?
Run to the Capitol, and nothing else?
And so return to you, and nothing else?

PORTIA
15 Yes, bring me word, boy, if thy lord look well,
For he went sickly forth; and take good note
What Caesar doth, what suitors press to him.
Hark, boy, what noise is that?

LUCIUS
I hear none, madam.

PORTIA
20 Prithee, listen well.
I heard a bustling rumor like a fray,
And the wind brings it from the Capitol.

---

10 *How . . . counsel* It is apparent that Brutus has revealed his secrets to Portia, as he
promised to do at the end of Act II, Scene i. But Portia's "manly resolution," as
demonstrated by the "voluntary wound" she has given herself "Here, in the thigh,"
seems to be breaking down in Act II, Scene iv, where she is much

ACT 2, SCENE 4

Rome, before the house of BRUTUS. PORTIA *and*
LUCIUS *enter.*

PORTIA
Boy, I beg you to run to the Senate House.
Don't wait to answer me, but get going.
Why are you waiting?

LUCIUS
To find out my errand, madam.

PORTIA
I would have liked you to go there and be back again   5
before I told you what you should do there.
(*aside*) Oh, self-control, be strong and help me!
Put a huge mountain between my heart and my tongue.
I have the mind of a man, but only the strength of a woman.
How hard it is for women to keep secrets!   10
(*to* LUCIUS) Are you still here?

LUCIUS
Madam, what am I supposed to do?
Run to the Capitol, and nothing else?
And then return to you, and nothing else?

PORTIA
Do this, boy—tell me whether your master looks well,   15
for he looked sick when he went out. And watch carefully
to see what Caesar does and what petitioners gather
    around him.
Listen, boy—what's that noise?

LUCIUS
I don't hear anything, madam.

PORTIA
Please, listen carefully.   20
I heard a chaotic sound, like a battle,
and the wind is bringing it from the Capitol.

---

troubled by the conflict of conventional male and female roles. The pressure of
events is finally too much for Portia, who becomes deranged and commits
suicide by swallowing live coals.

LUCIUS

Sooth, madam, I hear nothing.

Enter the SOOTHSAYER.

PORTIA

Come hither, fellow. Which way hast thou been?

SOOTHSAYER

25   At mine own house, good lady.

PORTIA

What is 't a clock?

SOOTHSAYER

About the ninth hour, lady.

PORTIA

Is Caesar yet gone to the Capitol?

SOOTHSAYER

Madam, not yet. I go to take my stand

30   To see him pass on to the Capitol.

PORTIA

Thou hast some suit to Caesar, hast thou not?

SOOTHSAYER

That I have, lady, if it will please Caesar
To be so good to Caesar as to hear me.
I shall beseech him to befriend himself.

PORTIA

35   Why, know'st thou any harm's intended towards him?

SOOTHSAYER

None that I know will be, much that I fear may chance.
Good morrow to you.—Here the street is narrow.
The throng that follows Caesar at the heels,
Of senators, of praetors, common suitors,

40   Will crowd a feeble man almost to death.
I'll get me to a place more void, and there
Speak to great Caesar as he comes along.

    Exit.

LUCIUS
Honestly, madam, I hear nothing.

The FORTUNE-TELLER *enters.*

PORTIA
Come here, fellow. Which way did you come from?

FORTUNE-TELLER
From my own house, good lady.   25

PORTIA
What time is it?

FORTUNE-TELLER
About nine o'clock, lady.

PORTIA
Has Caesar gone to the Capitol yet?

FORTUNE-TELLER
Not yet, madam. I'm going to find a place to stand
where I can see him pass on his way to the Capitol.   30

PORTIA
You have some request to make of Caesar, don't you?

FORTUNE-TELLER
Yes, I do, lady. If Caesar will only
do himself the favor of listening to me,
I shall beg him to be a friend to himself.

PORTIA
Why, do you know of any harm that's intended to him?   35

FORTUNE-TELLER
I don't know of anything certain, but I fear that much may
    happen.
Good morning to you. The street here is narrow.
The crowds of senators, judges, and common petitioners
that follow Caesar at his heels
would crush a weak man almost to death here.   40
I'll find myself a place less crowded, and there
I'll speak to great Caesar when he comes along.

    He exits.

PORTIA

I must go in. [*aside*] Ay me, how weak a thing
The heart of woman is! O Brutus,
45   The heavens speed thee in thine enterprise!
Sure the boy heard me. [*to* LUCIUS] Brutus hath a suit
That Caesar will not grant. [*aside*] O I grow faint.—
Run, Lucius, and commend me to my lord;
Say I am merry. Come to me again
50   And bring me word what he doth say to thee.

       Exeunt [*at different doors*].

PORTIA

    I must go inside. (*aside*) Oh, dear me, how weak a thing
    a woman's heart is! Oh, Brutus,
    may the heavens help you in your endeavor!   45
    But I'm sure the boy heard me say that. (*to* LUCIUS) Brutus
        has a request
    that Caesar will not grant. (*aside*) Oh, I grow faint.—
    Run, Lucius, and give my love to my lord.
    Tell him I am cheerful. Then come back to me
    and bring me word of what he said to you.   50

      They exit in different directions.

Act II Review

Discussion Questions

1. When Brutus says of Caesar, "I know no personal cause to spurn at him" and claims to be reluctant to kill him, how do we know that he is sincere?

2. Do you see any flaws or weaknesses in the conspirators' plans? Think about whether they have overlooked or underestimated anything as well as what the strengths of their plans might be. Explain your opinion.

3. Do you think the conspirators should have chosen a different leader? Name whom they might have chosen instead.

4. In Scene ii, Caesar says, "Cowards die many times before their deaths; / The valiant never taste of death but once." Explain what you think this famous line means, and then discuss the truth of the statement.

5. At the end of Act II, do you think Caesar has any inkling of his impending fate? Explain.

6. Many people warn Caesar against going to the Capitol on March 15. What do you think is the main reason Caesar decides to go despite all the warnings? Use evidence from both Acts I and II to support your response.

Literary Elements

1. In a **soliloquy** (a speech to himself) in Act II (Scene i, lines 10-34), Brutus states his doubts about attacking Caesar. What does Brutus consider good reasons for killing Caesar? You may have more than one answer.

2. **Irony** refers to the contrast between what appears to be and what actually is. In Scene i, Decius says, "But when I tell [Caesar] he hates flatterers, / He says he does, being then most flattered." Explain the irony.

3. What **motivates** Portia? List the many clues that Shakespeare provides in Act II, Scene i.

4. A **theme** is an author's ongoing topic, idea, or concern. The theme of sickness runs throughout Act II. Name some of the ways in which this idea is used. What point do you think Shakespeare makes by continually referring to this theme?

Writing Prompts

1. In Act II, Scene i, Metellus urges the other conspirators to bring Cicero on board in order to help "purchase us a good opinion / And buy men's voices to commend our deeds." Brutus also worries that killing Antony would make their "course . . . seem too bloody." At this stage of the conspiracy, what do you think a modern public relations firm would advise these men? Write out a plan that would maximize public approval of the revolt against Caesar and minimize public fallout. Include any special events you might plan, posters or fliers, public gifts or allowances, and so forth that would help your clients—the conspirators—prevail with confidence.

2. In Scene i, Brutus finds a mysterious letter on his bed that urges him to rise up against Caesar. Write a different version of this conspiratorial letter, one that uses facts and reasons instead of strange and emotional appeals. Why do you think Cassius chooses the latter form of communication to appeal to Brutus?

3. Julius Caesar is swayed by pressure from others in Act II, Scene ii. Write about a time someone influenced you. Explain how this person convinced you to act or think a certain way.

4. Brutus is forced to choose between his love for Caesar and his love for Rome. You, too, will face tough decisions, ones that have pros and cons. For example, think about what you might do in this situation: *Suppose your best friend has been nominated class treasurer. Your class will collect large sums of money for the homeless. You know that your friend has stolen money from an employer in the past. What do you do?* List the actions you could take and the pros and cons of each action. Then decide what action you would take, and explain your decision.

JULIUS CAESAR

ACT III

Marlon Brando, as Antony, addresses the crowd. Mankiewicz film, 1953

"FRIENDS, ROMANS, COUNTRYMEN,
LEND ME YOUR EARS; I COME TO BURY
CAESAR, NOT TO PRAISE HIM."

Before You Read

1. At this point, do you think the conspirators are justified in their intentions? Explain your answer.

2. What mistakes and miscalculations do you think the conspirators have made in their plans so far? Consider what their errors might lead to.

3. What role have women been playing in this story? Think about what role they might play in future events.

Literary Elements

1. Plots develop through **cause and effect**, or why things happen and what the results are. In Acts I and II, we see that the hatred Cassius and Casca feel for Caesar causes them to seek his downfall, so they send persuasive letters to Brutus. The effect is that Brutus joins them and an assassination plan begins.

2. An **inference** is a reasonable conclusion that the reader can draw based upon clues given in a work of literature. In Act I, Scene iii, Cassius says, "Poor man, I know he would not be a wolf / But that he sees the Romans are but sheep." We can infer that Cassius believes Caesar takes advantage of the Romans'—and here, Casca's—submissive attitude.

3. **Rhetoric** is the art of communicating effectively, either in writing or in speech. It uses persuasive techniques such as **repetition**, strong **imagery**, **rhythm**, **diction** (word choice), and **emotional appeals**, in addition to others. Look at the strongly worded letter—"Speak, strike, redress!"—Brutus receives in Act II, Scene i (lines 46–48) for an example.

4. Shakespeare often uses **repetition** to stress a character's emotions or traits or lend urgency to a theme or idea. In the beginning of Act I, Marullus scolds the cobbler for switching allegiance so rapidly from Pompey to Caesar. He harshens the rebuke by demanding, "And do you now put on your best attire? / And do you now cull out a holiday? And do you now strew flowers in his way . . . ?"

Words to Know

The following vocabulary words appear in Act III in the original text of Shakespeare's play. However, they are words that are still commonly used. Read the definitions here and pay attention to the words as you read the play (they will be in boldfaced type).

appeased	soothed; settled down
censure	judge; criticize
confounded	confused; overwhelmed
dint	force; impact
enfranchisement	end of slavery
extenuated	reduced; lessened
malice	hatred; cruelty
prostrate	lying face down; prone
unassailable	not open to attack; invulnerable
vanquished	beaten; defeated

Act Summary

On the ides of March, Caesar stands on the steps of the Capitol, surrounded by senators. In a haughty mood, he spurns Artemidorus's warning letter, claiming to put the Senate's business before any personal matters. He also rejects Metellus's petition for a pardon for his banished brother.

Seconds after Caesar grandly compares himself to Olympus, the home of the gods, Casca strikes him from behind, and his old friend Brutus attacks him from in front. Before dying, he cries out in shock: "*Et tu, Brutê?*—Then fall, Caesar!" The conspirators exclaim, "Liberty! Freedom! Tyranny is dead!" As an act of unity, they bathe their hands together in Caesar's blood.

Through a servant, Caesar's powerful friend Antony asks for permission to talk with the conspirators. Brutus assures him of the righteousness of their deed, while Cassius tries to sway Antony with promises of greater power. Antony asks to be allowed to give Caesar a eulogy at the public funeral ceremony. After the conspirators leave,

Antony vents his true feelings about Caesar's assassination. In his anger and grief, he vows to seek revenge.

The angry citizens demand an explanation of Caesar's death. Cassius goes off to address one crowd and Brutus another, repeating their charge against Caesar: He was ambitious, and his ambitions killed him. When it is his turn, Antony reminds the crowd of Caesar's devotion to them—why, he had planned in his will to make all the Roman citizens his heirs. Antony arouses them further by letting them view Caesar's blood-drenched corpse. He reminds them the deadly wounds came from men Caesar had thought were friends and allies. Now enraged, the crowds march on the homes of Brutus and the other conspirators and torch them. All of Caesar's assassins have to flee for their lives.

On his way to Caesar's funeral, Cinna the poet is stopped by a group of angry citizens. The mob confuses him with Cinna the conspirator and attacks him.

Charlton Heston as Mark Antony, Snells film, 1970

ACT III, SCENE I

[Rome. Before the Capitol]. Flourish. Enter CAESAR,
ANTONY, LEPIDUS, BRUTUS, CASSIUS, CASCA,
DECIUS, METELLUS, TREBONIUS, CINNA,
ARTEMIDORUS, PUBLIUS, [POPILIUS,] *the*
SOOTHSAYER *[and other* SENATORS *and* PETITIONERS].

CAESAR
The ides of March are come.

SOOTHSAYER
Ay, Caesar, but not gone.

ARTEMIDORUS
Hail, Caesar! Read this schedule.

DECIUS
Trebonius doth desire you to o'erread,
5   At your best leisure, this his humble suit.

ARTEMIDORUS
O Caesar, read mine first, for mine's a suit
That touches Caesar nearer. Read it, great Caesar.

CAESAR
What touches us ourself shall be last served.

ARTEMIDORUS
Delay not, Caesar, read it instantly.

CAESAR
10   What, is the fellow mad?

PUBLIUS
                              Sirrah, give place.

CASSIUS
What, urge you your petitions in the street?
Come to the Capitol.

        *[*CAESAR *enters the Capitol, the* OTHERS *following.]*

POPILIUS
I wish your enterprise today may thrive.

ACT 3, SCENE 1

Rome. Before the Capitol. Fanfare.

CAESAR, ANTONY, LEPIDUS, BRUTUS, CASSIUS, CASCA, DECIUS, METELLUS, TREBONIUS, CINNA, PUBLIUS, POPILIUS, ARTEMIDORUS, *the* FORTUNE-TELLER, *and other* SENATORS *and* PETITIONERS *enter.*

CAESAR
March 15 is here.

FORTUNE-TELLER
Yes, Caesar—but it's not over.

ARTEMIDORUS
Hail, Caesar. Read this paper.

DECIUS
Trebonius wants you to read
this humble petition whenever it best suits you.   5

ARTEMIDORUS
Oh, Caesar, read mine first—for my petition
concerns Caesar more urgently. Read it, great Caesar.

CAESAR
We'll save what concerns me personally for last.

ARTEMIDORUS
Don't delay, Caesar; read it instantly.

CAESAR
What, is the fellow mad?   10

PUBLIUS
Fellow, get out of the way.

CASSIUS
What, are you pushing your petitions in the street?
Come to the Capitol.

CAESAR and his FOLLOWERS enter the Capitol.

POPILIUS
I hope your endeavor goes well today.

CASSIUS

15   What enterprise, Popilius?

POPILIUS

Fare you well.

[*Advances to* CAESAR.]

BRUTUS

What said Popilius Lena?

CASSSIUS

He wished today our enterprise might thrive.
I fear our purpose is discovered.

BRUTUS

20   Look how he makes to Caesar. Mark him.

CASSIUS

Casca, be sudden, for we fear prevention.—
Brutus, what shall be done? If this be known,
Cassius or Caesar never shall turn back,
For I will slay myself.

BRUTUS

25   Cassius, be constant.
Popilius Lena speaks not of our purposes,
For look, he smiles, and Caesar doth not change.

CASSIUS

Trebonius knows his time, for look you, Brutus,
He draws Mark Antony out of the way.

[*Exeunt* ANTONY *and* TREBONIUS.]

DECIUS

30   Where is Metellus Cimber? Let him go
And presently prefer his suit to Caesar.

BRUTUS

He is addressed. Press near and second him.

CINNA

Casca, you are the first that rears your hand.

CAESAR

Are we all ready? What is now amiss

35   That Caesar and his Senate must redress?

CASSIUS
What endeavor, Popilius?   15

POPILIUS
Good-bye.

Walks up to CAESAR.

BRUTUS
What did Popilius Lena say?

CASSIUS
He said that he hoped our endeavor goes well today.
I'm afraid our plans have been discovered.

BRUTUS
Look—he's approaching Caesar. Watch him.   20

CASSIUS
Casca, act fast, for we're liable to be stopped.—
Brutus, what can we do? If our plans are known,
neither Cassius nor Caesar will return home alive,
for I will kill myself.

BRUTUS
Steady, Cassius.   25
Popilius Lena isn't saying anything about our plans,
for look—he's smiling, and Caesar's expression hasn't changed.

CASSIUS
Trebonius knows just when to act; look, Brutus—
he's leading Mark Antony out of the way.

TREBONIUS and ANTONY *exit.*

DECIUS
Where is Metellus Cimber? Let him go now   30
and present his petition to Caesar.

BRUTUS
He's ready. Stay close to him and back him up.

CINNA
Casca, you're to be the first to raise your hand.

CAESAR
Are we all ready? What things are wrong
that Caesar and his Senate must set right?   35

METELLUS [*kneeling*]

Most high, most mighty, and most puissant Caesar,
Metellus Cimber throws before thy seat
An humble heart.

CAESAR

                          I must prevent thee, Cimber.
40 These couchings and these lowly courtesies
    Might fire the blood of ordinary men
    And turn preordinance and first decree
    Into the law of children.* Be not fond
    To think that Caesar bears such rebel blood
45 That will be thawed from the true quality
    With that which melteth fools—I mean sweet words,
    Low-crooked curtsies, and base spaniel fawning.
    Thy brother by decree is banished.
    If thou dost bend and pray and fawn for him,
50 I spurn thee like a cur out of my way.
    Know, Caesar doth not wrong, nor without cause
    Will he be satisfied.

METELLUS

    Is there no voice more worthy than my own
    To sound more sweetly in great Caesar's ear
55 For the repealing of my banished brother?

BRUTUS [*kneeling*]

    I kiss thy hand, but not in flattery, Caesar,
    Desiring thee that Publius Cimber may
    Have an immediate freedom of repeal.

CAESAR

    What, Brutus?

CASSIUS [*kneeling*]

60   Pardon, Caesar; Caesar, pardon!
    As low as to thy foot doth Cassius fall
    To beg enfranchisement for Publius Cimber.

---

43 *law of children*   The phrase has religious overtones: i.e., the divinely ordained
    order of the universe is being converted into the merely capricious impulses that
    motivate children.

METELLUS (*kneeling*)

Most high, most mighty, and most powerful Caesar,
Metellus Cimber throws his humble heart
before your chair.

CAESAR

I must stop you, Cimber.
All this bowing and lowly flattery   40
might affect the blood of an ordinary man
and turn time-honored laws and decrees
into the rules of a children's game. Don't be so foolish
as to think that Caesar's emotions are so flighty
that his true firmness can be softened   45
by behavior which melts fools—I mean flattery;
low, stooping bows; and cringing, dog-like flattery.
Your brother, Publius Cimber, has been banished by decree.
If you bow, beg, and flatter for him,
I'll kick you out of my way like a dog.   50
Know that Caesar has done nothing unjust, nor will he grant a
      pardon
without good reason.

METELLUS

Won't someone with a voice more deserving than my own
speak more sweetly in great Caesar's ear
and ask him to call back my banished brother?   55

BRUTUS (*kneeling*)

I kiss your hand—but I'm not flattering you, Caesar.
I only ask that Publius Cimber
be allowed to return from exile.

CAESAR

What—you, Brutus?

CASSIUS (*kneeling*)

Pardon me, Caesar; Caesar, pardon me!   60
Cassius bows all the way down to your feet,
begging for Publius Cimber's freedom.

CAESAR
I could be well moved, if I were as you.
If I could pray to move, prayers would move me.
65 But I am constant as the Northern Star,
Of whose true-fixed and resting quality
There is no fellow in the firmament.
The skies are painted with unnumber'd sparks,
They are all fire, and every one doth shine;
70 But there's but one in all doth hold his place.
So in the world: 'tis furnished well with men,
And men are flesh and blood, and apprehensive;
Yet in the number I do know but one
That **unassailable** holds on his rank,
75 Unshaked of motion; and that I am he
Let me a little show it, even in this:
That I was constant Cimber should be banished,
And constant do remain to keep him so.

CINNA [*kneeling*]
O Caesar—

CAESAR
80   Hence! Wilt thou lift up Olympus?*

DECIUS [*kneeling*]
Great Caesar—

CAESAR
                    Doth not Brutus bootless kneel?

CASCA
Speak, hands, for me!
        They stab CAESAR.

CAESAR
Et tu, Brutè?—Then fall, Caesar.
        Dies.

CINNA
85 Liberty! Freedom! Tyranny is dead!
Run hence, proclaim, cry it about the streets.

---

80 *Olympus*   a mountain in Greece thought to be the home of the gods

CAESAR

> My mind could be changed if I were like you.
> If I could beg others to change their minds, your begging could
>   change my mind.
> But I am as immovable as the Northern Star,   65
> which has no equal in the sky
> in its fixed and unchanging nature.
> The sky is painted with countless stars;
> they're all made of fire, and every one shines.
> But there's only one star among them that stays in its place.   70
> So it is in the world; it is full of men,
> and men are made of flesh and blood and are capable of reason.
> But among them all, I know only one
> who invincibly holds on to his position,
> unmoved by any force; let me give a little proof   75
> that I am that man by how I act in this matter:
> I was determined that Cimber should be banished,
> and now I'm determined to keep him banished.

CINNA (*kneeling*)

> Oh, Caesar—

CAESAR

> Get away. Do you think you can lift up Olympus?   80

DECIUS (*kneeling*)

> Great Caesar—

CAESAR

> Didn't even Brutus find it useless to kneel?

CASCA

> Let my hands speak for me!

> > CASCA *stabs* CAESAR, *followed by the others;* BRUTUS *stabs*
> > CAESAR *last.*

CAESAR

> You too, Brutus? Then Caesar must die.

> > *He dies.*

CINNA

> Liberty! Freedom! Tyranny is dead!   85
> Run out, declare what we've done, cry it through the streets.

CASSIUS

Some to the common pulpits and cry out,
"Liberty, freedom, and **enfranchisement**!"

BRUTUS

People and senators, be not affrighted.
90 Fly not; stand still. Ambition's debt is paid.

CASCA

Go to the pulpit, Brutus.

DECIUS

And Cassius too.

BRUTUS

Where's Publius?

CINNA

Here, quite **confounded** with this mutiny.

METELLUS

95 Stand fast together, lest some friend of Caesar's
Should chance—

BRUTUS

Talk not of standing.—Publius, good cheer,
There is no harm intended to your person,
Nor to no Roman else. So tell them, Publius.

CASSIUS

100 And leave us, Publius, lest that the people,
Rushing on us, should do your age some mischief.

BRUTUS

Do so; and let no man abide this deed
But we the doers.

[*All but the* CONSPIRATORS *exit.*] *Enter* TREBONIUS.

CASSIUS

Where is Antony?

TREBONIUS

105 Fled to his house amazed.
Men, wives, and children stare, cry out, and run,
As it were doomsday.

CASSIUS

Some of you, go to the public speaking platforms and cry out,
"Liberty, freedom, and the end of slavery!"

BRUTUS

People and senators, don't be afraid.
Don't run away; hold still. An ambitious man has gotten what   90
he deserved.

CASCA

Go to the speaking platform, Brutus.

DECIUS

And Cassius, too.

BRUTUS

Where's Publius?

CINNA

Here—completely overwhelmed by this uproar.

METELLUS

Stand close together, in case some friend of Caesar's   95
should happen to—

BRUTUS

Let's not talk of defending ourselves.—Publius, don't worry.
No one intends any harm to you
or to any other Roman. So tell that to the people, Publius.

CASSIUS

And leave us, Publius—for the people   100
might hurt an old man like you if they rush upon us.

BRUTUS

Do so—and let no man face the consequences of this deed
except those of us who did it.

> *All but the* CONSPIRATORS *exit;* TREBONIUS *enters.*

CASSIUS

Where is Antony?

TREBONIUS

He's fled to his house, stunned.   105
Men, wives, and children stare, scream, and run around
as if it were the end of the world.

BRUTUS

Fates, we will know your pleasures.
That we shall die, we know; 'tis but the time,
And drawing days out, that men stand upon.

CASCA

Why, he that cuts off twenty years of life
Cuts off so many years of fearing death.

BRUTUS

Grant that, and then is death a benefit.
So are we Caesar's friends, that have abridged
His time of fearing death. Stoop, Romans, stoop,
And let us bathe our hands in Caesar's blood
Up to the elbows and besmear our swords.
Then walk we forth, even to the marketplace,
And waving our red weapons o'er our heads,
Let's all cry, "Peace, freedom, and liberty!"

CASSIUS

Stoop then, and wash.

[*They smear their hands and swords with* CAESAR'*s blood.*]

How many ages hence
Shall this our lofty scene be acted over,
In states unborn and accents yet unknown!

BRUTUS

How many times shall Caesar bleed in sport,
That now on Pompey's basis lies along
No worthier than the dust!

CASSIUS

So oft as that shall be,
So often shall the knot of us be called
The men that gave their country liberty.

DECIUS

What, shall we forth?

CASSIUS

Ay, every man away.
Brutus shall lead, and we will grace his heels
With the most boldest and best hearts of Rome.

BRUTUS

Fates, sooner or later we'll learn your will.
We know that we must die; men only really care about
the times of their deaths and prolonging their lives. 110

CASCA

Why, a man who cuts twenty years off his life
cuts off that many years of fearing death.

BRUTUS

If we accept that as true, then death is a kindness.
So we are Caesar's friends, because we have shortened
his time of fearing death. Stoop down, Romans, stoop down, 115
and let us bathe our hands in Caesar's blood
up to the elbows and smear it on our swords.
Then let's walk out, all the way to the marketplace,
and waving our red swords over our heads,
let's all cry, "Peace, freedom, and liberty!" 120

CASCA

Stoop down, then, and let's bathe in blood.

They smear their hands and swords with CAESAR's *blood.*

In how many future ages
will this noble scene be reenacted again and again—
in nations not yet founded and languages not yet known!

BRUTUS

How many times will Caesar bleed as part of a play—
lying as he does now at the base of Pompey's statue, 125
worth no more than dust!

CASSIUS

Whenever that happens,
this little group of ours will be called
the men who gave their country liberty.

DECIUS

But shouldn't we leave the Capitol? 130

CASSIUS

Yes, let's all of us go.
Brutus will lead us—and we, the bravest and best hearts of Rome,
will do him the honor of following him.

Enter a SERVANT.

BRUTUS
Soft, who comes here? A friend of Antony's.

SERVANT
135 Thus, Brutus, did my master bid me kneel.
Thus did Mark Antony bid me fall down,
And being **prostrate**, thus he bade me say:
Brutus is noble, wise, valiant, and honest;
Caesar was mighty, bold, royal, and loving.
140 Say, I love Brutus and I honor him;
Say, I feared Caesar, honored him, and loved him.
If Brutus will vouchsafe that Antony
May safely come to him, and be resolved
How Caesar hath deserved to lie in death,
145 Mark Antony shall not love Caesar dead
So well as Brutus living; but will follow
The fortunes and affairs of noble Brutus
Thorough the hazards of this untrod state
With all true faith. So says my master Antony.

BRUTUS
150 Thy master is a wise and valiant Roman;
I never thought him worse.
Tell him, so please him come unto this place,
He shall be satisfied and, by my honor,
Depart untouched.

SERVANT
155   I'll fetch him presently.

Exit SERVANT.

BRUTUS
I know that we shall have him well to friend.

CASSIUS
I wish we may. But yet have I a mind
That fears him much, and my misgiving still
Falls shrewdly to the purpose.

Enter ANTONY.

A SERVANT *enters.*

BRUTUS

Wait, who's coming? It's a friend of Antony's.

SERVANT

(*kneeling*) My master told me to kneel like this, Brutus.   135
Mark Antony told me to fall on my knees like this,
and once I had fallen down, he told me to say this:
"Brutus is noble, wise, brave, and honorable;
Caesar was mighty, bold, generous, and loving.
Tell Brutus I love him, and that I honor him;   140
tell him I respected Caesar, honored him, and loved him.
If Brutus will allow Antony
to come to him safely and receive a satisfactory explanation
concerning why Caesar deserved to be killed,
Mark Antony will not love the dead Caesar   145
as much as he does the living Brutus; and he will ally himself
with noble Brutus's destiny and business
with complete loyalty, through all the dangers
of this still uncertain state of affairs." This is what my master
    Antony says.

BRUTUS

Your master is a wise, brave Roman.   150
I never thought him to be worse.
Tell him that, if he'll kindly come to this place,
he'll receive a satisfactory explanation; and I promise on my honor
that he'll leave unharmed.

SERVANT

I'll bring him right away.   155

    The SERVANT *exits.*

BRUTUS

I'm sure that Antony will be a good friend to us.

CASSIUS

I hope so. But in my mind,
I fear him a great deal, and my worries
always turn out to be justified.

    ANTONY *enters.*

BRUTUS

160   But here comes Antony.—Welcome, Mark Antony.

ANTONY

        O mighty Caesar! Dost thou lie so low?
        Are all thy conquests, glories, triumphs, spoils,
        Shrunk to this little measure? Fare thee well.—
        I know not, gentlemen, what you intend,
165   Who else must be let blood, who else is rank.
        If I myself, there is no hour so fit
        As Caesar's death's hour; nor no instrument
        Of half that worth as those your swords made rich
        With the most noble blood of all this world.
170   I do beseech ye, if you bear me hard,
        Now, whilst your purpled hands do reek and smoke,
        Fulfill your pleasure. Live a thousand years,
        I shall not find myself so apt to die.
        No place will please me so, no mean of death,
175   As here by Caesar, and by you cut off,
        The choice and master spirits of this age.

BRUTUS

        O Antony! Beg not your death of us.
        Though now we must appear bloody and cruel,
        As by our hands and this our present act
180   You see we do; yet see you but our hands,
        And this the bleeding business they have done.
        Our hearts you see not; they are pitiful;
        And pity to the general wrong of Rome—
        As fire drives out fire, so pity pity—*
185   Hath done this deed on Caesar. For your part,
        To you our swords have leaden points, Mark Antony.
        Our arms in strength of **malice**, and our hearts
        Of brothers' temper, do receive you in
        With all kind love, good thoughts, and reverence.

CASSIUS

190   Your voice shall be as strong as any man's
        In the disposing of new dignities.

---

184   *As fire . . . pity*   proverbial formulas. "Pity to the general wrong of Rome" has
      driven out pity for Caesar, who was the cause of Rome's plight.

BRUTUS

But here comes Antony.—Welcome, Mark Antony!   160

ANTONY (*addressing the dead* CAESAR)

Oh, mighty Caesar, do you lie so low?
Have all your conquests, glories, triumphs, and spoils of war
been shrunken down to such a little space? Farewell.—
Gentlemen, I don't know what you intend to do—
who else must be killed, who else has grown too powerful.   165
If you mean to kill me, there's no better hour for it
than the hour of Caesar's death—nor any weapons
half as worthy as those swords of yours, enriched
by the noblest blood in all this world.
I beg you, if you have a grudge against me,   170
do what you mean to do right now, while your reddened hands
are still steaming with fresh blood. If I should live a thousand
      years,
I'll never feel so ready to die.
No place could please me better, nor any other kind of death,
than to die here beside Caesar—and to be killed by you,   175
the elite, ruling spirits of this time.

BRUTUS

Oh, Antony, do not beg us to kill you!
We must now seem murderous and cruel to you,
judging from our bloody hands and this deed
you see that we've done; and yet you only see our hands   180
and the bloody business they have carried out.
You do not see our hearts; they are full of pity;
and our pity for the wronged people of Rome
caused us to kill Caesar—for just as fire
can put out fire, pity can put out pity. Toward you,   185
Mark Antony, the points of our swords are blunt.
Our arms, made strong by this deed, and our hearts,
full of brotherly feeling, are ready to embrace you
with kind love, good thoughts, and respect.

CASSIUS

You'll have as much influence as any other man   190
when it comes to granting power to others.

BRUTUS

Only be patient till we have **appeased**
The multitude, beside themselves with fear,
And then we will deliver you the cause
195 Why I, that did love Caesar when I struck him,
Have thus proceeded.

ANTONY

                    I doubt not of your wisdom.
Let each man render me his bloody hand.
First, Marcus Brutus, will I shake with you.—
200 Next, Caius Cassius, do I take your hand.—
Now, Decius Brutus, yours;—now yours, Metellus;—
Yours, Cinna; —and, my valiant Casca, yours.
Though last, not least in love, yours, good Trebonius.
Gentlemen all—alas, what shall I say?
205 My credit now stands on such slippery ground
That one of two bad ways you must conceit me,
Either a coward or a flatterer.
That I did love thee, Caesar, O 'tis true!
If then thy spirit look upon us now,
210 Shall it not grieve thee dearer than thy death
To see thy Antony making his peace,
Shaking the bloody fingers of thy foes—
Most noble!—in the presence of thy corse?
Had I as many eyes as thou hast wounds,
215 Weeping as fast as they stream forth thy blood,
It would become me better than to close
In terms of friendship with thine enemies.
Pardon me, Julius! Here wast thou bayed, brave hart;*
Here didst thou fall; and here thy hunters stand
220 Signed in thy spoil, and crimsoned in thy Lethe.
O world, thou wast the forest to this hart,
And this indeed, O world, the heart of thee!
How like a deer, strucken by many princes,
Dost thou here lie!

CASSIUS

225 Mark Antony—

---

218   *hart*   wordplay on "hart/heart." "Hart" is the adult male deer, usually the red
deer.

BRUTUS
For now, be patient until we have calmed
the people, who are beside themselves with fear;
and then we will tell you the reason
why I, who loved Caesar even when I stabbed him,   195
have done what I have done.

ANTONY
I don't question your wisdom.
Let each of you give me his bloody hand.
First, Marcus Brutus, I will shake hands with you.—
Next, Caius Cassius, I will take your hand.—   200
Now, Decius Brutus, I take yours.—Now yours, Metellus.—
And yours, Cinna.—And my brave Casca, yours.—
And last, but not least in my love, yours, good Trebonius.—
Gentlemen that you all are—alas, what can I say?
My reputation now stands on such slippery ground   205
that you must judge me in one of two bad ways,
as either a coward or a flatterer.—
Oh, Caesar, it's true that I loved you!
If your spirit is looking upon us now,
won't it cause you even more grief than your death   210
to see your Antony making peace,
shaking the bloody hands of your enemies—
your noble enemies!—in the presence of your corpse?
If I had as many eyes as you have wounds,
weeping tears as fast as your wounds pour out blood,   215
it would suit me better than to unite
in friendship with your enemies.
Pardon me, Julius! Here you were hunted down, brave hart;
here you fell; and here your hunters stand—
marked by your destruction, stained red by your life's blood.   220
Oh, world, you were the forest to this deer,
and, oh, world, Caesar was truly your dear one.
And now you lie here, so much like a deer
wounded by many princes!

CASSIUS
Mark Antony—

ANTONY

>   Pardon me, Caius Cassius.
>   The enemies of Caesar shall say this;
>   Then, in a friend, it is cold modesty.

CASSIUS

>   I blame you not for praising Caesar so,
> 230 But what compact mean you to have with us?
>   Will you be pricked* in number of our friends,
>   Or shall we on and not depend on you?

ANTONY

>   Therefore I took your hands, but was indeed
>   Swayed from the point by looking down on Caesar.
> 235 Friends am I with you all, and love you all,
>   Upon this hope, that you shall give me reasons
>   Why and wherein Caesar was dangerous.

BRUTUS

>   Or else were this a savage spectacle.
>   Our reasons are so full of good regard
> 240 That were you, Antony, the son of Caesar,
>   You should be satisfied.

ANTONY

>   That's all I seek,
>   And am, moreover, suitor that I may
>   Produce his body to the marketplace,
> 245 And in the pulpit, as becomes a friend,
>   Speak in the order of his funeral.

BRUTUS

>   You shall, Mark Antony.

CASSIUS

>   Brutus, a word with you.
>   [aside to BRUTUS] You know not what you do. Do not
> 250   consent
>   That Antony speak in his funeral.
>   Know you how much the people may be moved
>   By that which he will utter?

---

231   *pricked*   marked down, by making a pinhole or dot next to the name on a list

ANTONY

Pardon me, Caius Cassius.
Caesar's enemies are going to say this, too—
so it's not excessive for a friend to say it.

CASSIUS

I don't blame you for praising Caesar like that.
But what agreement do you intend to make with us?   230
Can we count you among our friends,
or should we proceed and not depend on you?

ANTONY

That's why I took your hands—but indeed,
I was distracted from the point when I looked down at Caesar.
I am a friend to you all and love you all,   235
and hope that you will tell me the reasons
why and how Caesar was so dangerous.

BRUTUS

Otherwise, this would be a savage sight.
Our reasons were so well-considered,
Antony, that even if you were Caesar's son   240
you would be satisfied by them.

ANTONY

That's all I hope for,
and moreover, I ask your permission
to present his body in the marketplace,
and as befits a friend, to speak on the platform   245
during his funeral ceremonies.

BRUTUS

You shall, Mark Antony.

CASSIUS

Brutus, I want a word with you.
(*aside to* BRUTUS) You don't know what you're doing.
    Don't allow   250
Antony to speak at his funeral.
Don't you know how much the people might be moved
by what he'll have to say?

BRUTUS [*aside to CASSIUS*]

                                 By your pardon—
255 I will myself into the pulpit first,
And show the reason of our Caesar's death.
What Antony shall speak, I will protest
He speaks by leave and by permission;
And that we are contented Caesar shall
260 Have all true rites and lawful ceremonies,
It shall advantage more than do us wrong.

CASSIUS [*aside to BRUTUS*]
I know not what may fall. I like it not.

BRUTUS
Mark Antony, here, take you Caesar's body.
You shall not in your funeral speech blame us,
265 But speak all good you can devise of Caesar
And say you do 't by our permission.
Else shall you not have any hand at all
About his funeral. And you shall speak
In the same pulpit whereto I am going,
270 After my speech is ended.

ANTONY
                                 Be it so;
I do desire no more.

BRUTUS
Prepare the body, then, and follow us.

          Exeunt. ANTONY *remains.*

ANTONY
O pardon me, thou bleeding piece of earth,
275 That I am meek and gentle with these butchers.
Thou art the ruins of the noblest man
That ever lived in the tide of times.
Woe to the hand that shed this costly blood!
Over thy wounds now do I prophesy
280 (Which like dumb mouths do ope their ruby lips
To beg the voice and utterance of my tongue),
A curse shall light upon the limbs of men;
Domestic fury and fierce civil strife
Shall cumber all the parts of Italy;

BRUTUS (*to* CASSIUS)
Don't worry,
I'll go to the platform first   255
and explain our reasons for killing Caesar.
When Antony is ready to speak, I will declare
that he speaks with our permission,
and that we will be happy for Caesar
to have all the proper services and lawful ceremonies.   260
This will do us more good than harm.

CASSIUS (*to* BRUTUS)
I don't know what might happen. I don't like it.

BRUTUS
Here, Mark Antony—take Caesar's body.
You may not blame us in your funeral speech,
but say everything good you can think of about Caesar,   265
and also say that you do so with our permission.
Otherwise, you won't be able to take part
in his funeral at all. And you will speak
on the same platform where I'm speaking,
after my speech has ended.   270

ANTONY
That's fine.
I want nothing else.

BRUTUS
Then prepare the body and follow us.

> *Everyone but* ANTONY *exits.*

ANTONY (*addressing* CAESAR's *body*)
Oh, pardon me, you bleeding piece of earth,
for being meek and gentle with these butchers.   275
You are the ruins of the noblest man
who ever lived throughout the course of history.
Woe to the hand that shed this precious blood!
Your wounds open their red lips like silent mouths,
begging my tongue to speak for them;   280
and over your wounds, I prophesy
that a curse will fall upon all men's undertakings;
all parts of Italy will be overwhelmed

285 Blood and destruction shall be so in use
And dreadful objects so familiar,
That mothers shall but smile when they behold
Their infants quartered with the hands of war,
All pity choked with custom of fell deeds;
290 And Caesar's spirit, ranging for revenge,
With Até* by his side come hot from hell,
Shall in these confines with a monarch's voice
Cry "Havoc!" and let slip the dogs of war,
That this foul deed shall smell above the earth
295 With carrion men, groaning for burial.

Enter Octavius's SERVANT.

You serve Octavius Caesar, do you not?

SERVANT
I do, Mark Antony.

ANTONY
Caesar did write for him to come to Rome.

SERVANT
He did receive his letters and is coming,
300 And bid me to say to you by word of mouth—
O Caesar!

ANTONY
Thy heart is big; get thee apart and weep.
Passion I see is catching, for mine eyes,
Seeing those beds of sorrow stand in thine,
305 Began to water. Is thy master coming?

SERVANT
He lies tonight within seven leagues of Rome.

ANTONY
Post back with speed and tell him what hath chanced.
Here is a mourning Rome, a dangerous Rome,
No Rome of safety for Octavius yet;
310 Hie hence and tell him so.—Yet stay awhile;
Thou shalt not back till I have borne this corpse

---

291 *Até* Greek goddess of discord and vengeance

by civil disturbances and war;   285
blood and destruction will become so common,
and horrible sights so routine,
that mothers will only smile when they see
their babies hacked to pieces by soldiers—
for cruel deeds will be so frequent that pity will be destroyed.
And Caesar's spirit will go forth seeking revenge—   290
with Até at his side, hot from hell;
and throughout these regions, he'll cry out in a kingly voice,
"No prisoners!" and unleash the dogs of war
so that this foul deed will stink throughout the world,
along with dead and rotting men groaning to be buried.   295

>   *Octavius's* SERVANT *enters.*

You serve Octavius Caesar, don't you?

SERVANT
I do, Mark Antony.

ANTONY
Caesar wrote to him, telling him to come to Rome.

SERVANT
He received Caesar's letters and is coming
and asked me tell you—   300
(*seeing the body*) Oh, Caesar!

ANTONY
Your heart swells with grief. Go aside and weep.
I see that emotion is catching, for my eyes,
upon seeing those tears in your eyes,
are beginning to water. Is your master coming?   305

SERVANT
Tonight he is within seven leagues of Rome.

ANTONY
Ride quickly back to him, and tell him what has happened.
Rome is mourning, Rome is dangerous—
and Rome is not yet safe for Octavius.
Go and tell him so.—But no, stay here awhile;   310
you'll not go back until I have carried this corpse

Into the marketplace. There I shall try,
In my oration, how the people take
The cruel issue of these bloody men,
315   According to the which thou shalt discourse
To young Octavius of the state of things.
Lend me your hand.

        Exeunt [*with* CAESAR'S *body*].

to the marketplace. In my oration there,
I'll test how the people react
to the cruel deed done by these murderous men;
and according to what I learn, you'll be able to tell 315
young Octavius the state of things here in Rome.
Give me a hand.

They exit with CAESAR'S *body.*

ACT III, SCENE II

[*Rome. The Forum.*] *Enter* BRUTUS *and* CASSIUS, *with the* PLEBEIANS.

PLEBEIANS
We will be satisfied! Let us be satisfied!

BRUTUS
Then follow me and give me audience, friends.
Cassius, go you into the other street
And part the numbers.—
Those that will hear me speak, let 'em stay here;
Those that will follow Cassius, go with him;
And public reasons shall be rendered
Of Caesar's death.

FIRST PLEBEIAN
                    I will hear Brutus speak.

SECOND PLEBEIAN
I will hear Cassius, and compare their reasons
When severally we hear them rendered.

[*Exit* CASSIUS, *with some of the* PLEBIANS.] BRUTUS *goes into the pulpit.*

THIRD PLEBEIAN
The noble Brutus is ascended. Silence!

BRUTUS
Be patient till the last.
Romans, countrymen, and lovers, hear me for my cause, and be silent, that you may hear. Believe me for mine honor, and have respect to mine honor, that you may believe. **Censure** me in your wisdom, and awake your senses, that you may the better judge. If there be any in this assembly, any dear friends of Caesar's, to him I say that Brutus's love to Caesar was no less than his. If then that friend demand why Brutus rose against Caesar, this is my answer: not that I loved Caesar less, but that I loved Rome more. Had you rather Caesar were living, and die all slaves, than that Caesar were dead, to live all freemen? As Caesar loved me, I weep for him; as he was fortunate, I

ACT 3, SCENE 2

The Forum. BRUTUS *and* CASSIUS *enter with a mob of ordinary*
CITIZENS.

CITIZENS
We demand an explanation! Give us an explanation!

BRUTUS
Then come along and listen to me, friends.—
Cassius, go to the other street
and divide the crowd.—
Those of you who want to hear me speak, stay right here;   5
those of you who'd rather listen to Cassius, go with him;
and we'll make public our reasons
for Caesar's death.

FIRST CITIZEN
I want to hear Brutus speak.

SECOND CITIZEN
I'll go listen to Cassius; we'll compare their reasons   10
after we've heard what they say separately.

> CASSIUS *exits with some of the* CITIZENS. BRUTUS *goes up to*
> *the platform.*

THIRD CITIZEN
The noble Brutus has gone up on the platform. Be quiet.

BRUTUS
Be patient until I'm finished.
Romans, countrymen, and dear friends—listen to my grounds
for action, and be quiet so that you can hear me. Believe me   15
because I'm honorable, and accept me as an honorable man so
you'll believe me. Judge me with all your wisdom, and put all
your reasoning powers to work so you can judge me better. If
there is any dear friend of Caesar's in this crowd, I tell him that
Brutus's love for Caesar was no less than his. If that friend   20
demands to know why Brutus rose up against Caesar, this is
my answer: not that I loved Caesar less, but that I loved Rome
more. Would you rather Caesar were alive and all of you were
to die slaves, than to have Caesar dead and to live as free men?
Because Caesar loved me, I weep for him. Because he was   25

rejoice at it; as he was valiant, I honor him; but, as he was ambitious, I slew him. There is tears for his love; joy for his fortune; honor for his valor; and death for his ambition. Who is here so base that would be a bondman? If any, speak; for him have I offended. Who is here so rude that would not be a Roman? If any, speak; for him have I offended. Who is here so vile that will not love his country? If any, speak; for him have I offended. I pause for a reply.

ALL
None, Brutus, none.

BRUTUS
Then none have I offended. I have done no more to Caesar than you shall do to Brutus. The question of his death is enrolled in the Capitol; his glory not **extenuated**, wherein he was worthy; nor his offenses enforced, for which he suffered death.

Enter MARK ANTONY with CAESAR'S body.

Here comes his body, mourned by Mark Antony, who, though he had no hand in his death, shall receive the benefit of his dying—a place in the commonwealth—as which of you shall not? With this I depart: that, as I slew my best lover for the good of Rome, I have the same dagger for myself when it shall please my country to need my death.

ALL
Live, Brutus! Live, live!

FIRST PLEBEIAN
Bring him with triumph home unto his house.

SECOND PLEBEIAN
Give him a statue with his ancestors.

THIRD PLEBEIAN
Let him be Caesar.

FOURTH PLEBEIAN
                    Caesar's better parts
Shall be crowned in Brutus.

lucky, I rejoice for him. Because he was brave, I respect him. But because he was ambitious, I killed him. Here are tears for his love, joy for his luck, respect for his bravery, and death for his ambition. Is there anyone here despicable enough to want to be a slave? If there is, let him speak up, for I have offended him. Is there anyone here uncivilized enough not to want to be a Roman? If there is, let him speak up, for I have offended him. Is there anyone here so villainous that he doesn't love his country? If there is, let him speak up, for I have offended him. I wait for a reply.

CITIZENS

None of us, Brutus, none of us. 35

BRUTUS

Then I have offended none of you. I haven't done anything more to Caesar than you would do to Brutus under the same circumstances. The reasons for his death are written on a scroll in the Capitol; the glories that he earned are not minimized, nor are the offenses that led to his death exaggerated. 40

MARK ANTONY *and others enter with* CAESAR'S *body.*

Here comes his body, mourned by Mark Antony. Although he played no part in Caesar's death, Antony will benefit from it by a government position. And which of you won't benefit, as well? Before I leave, let me say this: Just as I killed my best 45 friend for the good of Rome, I've got the same dagger ready for myself if my country should ever want me to die.

CITIZENS

Long live Brutus! Long live Brutus!

FIRST CITIZEN

Carry him like a hero to his house.

SECOND CITIZEN

Erect a statue of him alongside the statues of his ancestors. 50

THIRD CITIZEN

Let him be the new Caesar.

FOURTH CITIZEN

Caesar's best qualities
will be crowned with Brutus.

FIRST PLEBEIAN
We'll bring him to his house with shouts and clamors.

BRUTUS
55   My countrymen—

SECOND PLEBEIAN
Peace! Silence! Brutus speaks.

FIRST PLEBEIAN
Peace, ho!

BRUTUS
Good countrymen, let me depart alone,
And, for my sake, stay here with Antony.
60   Do grace to Caesar's corpse, and grace his speech
Tending to Caesar's glories, which Mark Antony,
By our permission, is allowed to make.
I do entreat you, not a man depart
Save I alone, till Antony have spoke.

        Exit.

FIRST PLEBEIAN
65   Stay, ho! And let us hear Mark Antony.

THIRD PLEBEIAN
Let him go up into the public chair.

PLEBIEANS
We'll hear him.—Noble Antony, go up.

ANTONY
For Brutus's sake, I am beholding to you.

FOURTH PLEBIAN
What does he say of Brutus?

THIRD PLEBEIAN
70   He says, for Brutus's sake
He finds himself beholding to us all.

FOURTH PLEBEIAN
'Twere best he speak no harm of Brutus here!

FIRST PLEBEIAN
This Caesar was a tyrant.

FIRST CITIZEN
We'll take him to his house with noise and shouting.

BRUTUS
My countrymen— 55

SECOND CITIZEN
Quiet, silence! Brutus is speaking.

FIRST CITIZEN
Quiet, listen!

BRUTUS
Good countrymen, let me depart by myself—
and for my sake, stay here with Antony.
Honor Caesar's corpse, and listen respectfully to his speech 60
about Caesar's glories, for he has been allowed
to speak with our permission.
I beg you—until Antony has spoken,
let no man leave except myself.

He comes down from the platform and exits.

FIRST CITIZEN
Let's stay, then, and listen to Mark Antony! 65

THIRD CITIZEN
Let him go up to the speaking platform.
We'll listen to him. Noble Antony, go on up.

ANTONY
For Brutus's sake, I am indebted to you.

He goes up to the platform.

FOURTH CITIZEN
What did he say about Brutus?

THIRD CITIZEN
He said that, for Brutus's sake, 70
he found himself indebted to us all.

FOURTH CITIZEN
He'd better not say anything bad about Brutus here.

FIRST CITIZEN
Caesar was a tyrant.

THIRD PLEBEIAN

                           Nay, that's certain.
75   We are blest that Rome is rid of him.

SECOND PLEBEIAN

Peace! Let us hear what Antony can say.

ANTONY

You gentle Romans—

ALL

                     Peace, ho! Let us hear him.

ANTONY

Friends, Romans, countrymen, lend me your ears.
80   I come to bury Caesar, not to praise him.
The evil that men do lives after them,
The good is oft interred with their bones;
So let it be with Caesar. The noble Brutus
Hath told you Caesar was ambitious.
85   If it were so, it was a grievous fault,
And grievously hath Caesar answered it.
Here, under leave of Brutus and the rest—
For Brutus is an honorable man;
So are they all, all honorable men—
90   Come I to speak in Caesar's funeral.
He was my friend, faithful and just to me,
But Brutus says he was ambitious,
And Brutus is an honorable man.
He hath brought many captives home to Rome,
95   Whose ransoms did the general coffers fill.
Did this in Caesar seem ambitious?
When that the poor have cried, Caesar hath wept.
Ambition should be made of sterner stuff,
Yet Brutus says he was ambitious;
100 And Brutus is an honorable man.
You all did see that on the Lupercal
I thrice presented him a kingly crown,
Which he did thrice refuse. Was this ambition?
Yet Brutus says he was ambitious;
105 And sure he is an honorable man.
I speak not to disprove what Brutus spoke,

THIRD CITIZEN
That's certainly true.
We are blessed that Rome is rid of him. 75

SECOND CITIZEN
Quiet, let's hear what Antony has to say.

ANTONY
You noble Romans—

CITIZENS
Quiet, listen! Let's hear him.

ANTONY
Friends, Romans, countrymen, give me your attention.
I've come to bury Caesar, not to praise him. 80
The evil that men do is remembered after they die,
while the good they do is often buried with their bones.
Let it be the same with Caesar. The noble Brutus
has told you that Caesar was ambitious.
If that's true, it was a terrible fault, 85
and Caesar has paid a high price for it.
With the permission of Brutus and the others,
I have come here to speak at Caesar's funeral
(for Brutus is an honorable man;
so are the rest of them—they are all honorable men). 90
Caesar was my friend—loyal and just to me;
but Brutus says he was ambitious,
and Brutus is an honorable man.
Caesar brought many captives home to Rome,
whose ransoms filled the public treasury. 95
Did this seem ambitious of Caesar?
When the poor cried, Caesar wept, too;
ambitious men should be tougher than that.
Still, Brutus says he was ambitious,
and Brutus is an honorable man. 100
You all saw how, during the feast of Lupercal,
I offered him a kingly crown three times,
and he refused to take it every time. Was that ambitious?
Still, Brutus says he was ambitious,
and Brutus is certainly an honorable man. 105
I'm not saying any of this to disprove what Brutus said,

But here I am to speak what I do know.
You all did love him once, not without cause;
What cause withholds you then to mourn for him?
110 O judgment! Thou art fled to brutish beasts,
And men have lost their reason.—Bear with me;
My heart is in the coffin there with Caesar,
And I must pause till it come back to me.

[*He weeps.*]

FIRST PLEBEIAN
Methinks there is much reason in his sayings.

SECOND PLEBEIAN
115 If thou consider rightly of the matter,
Caesar has had great wrong.

THIRD PLEBEIAN
                                        Has he, masters?
I fear there will a worse come in his place.

FOURTH PLEBEIAN
Marked ye his words? He would not take the crown;
120 Therefore 'tis certain he was not ambitious.

FIRST PLEBEIAN
If it be found so, some will dear abide it.

SECOND PLEBEIAN
Poor soul, his eyes are red as fire with weeping.

THIRD PLEBEIAN
There's not a nobler man in Rome than Antony.

FOURTH PLEBEIAN
Now mark him, he begins again to speak.

ANTONY
125 But yesterday, the word of Caesar might
Have stood against the world. Now lies he there,
And none so poor to do him reverence.
O masters! If I were disposed to stir
Your hearts and minds to mutiny and rage,
130 I should do Brutus wrong and Cassius wrong,
Who, you all know, are honorable men.
I will not do them wrong. I rather choose

but only to tell you what I know.
You all loved him once, and not without good cause.
So what cause do you have now to not mourn his death?—
Oh, wisdom now belongs only to savage beasts, 110
and men have lost their powers of reason! Be patient with me;
my heart is in the coffin with Caesar,
and I must pause to get control of my emotions.

He weeps.

FIRST CITIZEN
I think there's much good sense in what he says.

SECOND CITIZEN
If you think it over carefully, 115
Caesar was badly wronged.

THIRD CITIZEN
Was he, friends?
I'm afraid that even worse wrongs are on the way.

FOURTH CITIZEN
Did you hear what he said? Caesar wouldn't take the crown;
so it's certain that he wasn't ambitious. 120

FIRST CITIZEN
If that proves true, some people will pay dearly for his death.

SECOND CITIZEN
Poor soul—Antony's eyes are as red as fire from weeping.

THIRD CITIZEN
There's a not a nobler man in Rome than Antony.

FOURTH CITIZEN
Now listen to him. He's starting to speak again.

ANTONY
Only yesterday, just a word from Caesar might 125
have challenged the world. Now he lies there,
and no one is humble enough to honor him.
Oh, masters, if I wanted to stir
your hearts and minds to rebellion and rage,
I would do wrong to Brutus and Cassius— 130
who are, as you all know, honorable men.
I will not do them wrong. Instead, I choose

To wrong the dead, to wrong myself and you,
Than I will wrong such honorable men.
135 But here's a parchment with the seal of Caesar;
I found it in his closet. 'Tis his will.
Let but the commons hear this testament,
Which, pardon me, I do not mean to read,
And they would go and kiss dead Caesar's wounds,
140 And dip their napkins in his sacred blood—
Yea, beg a hair of him for memory,
And, dying, mention it within their wills,
Bequeathing it as a rich legacy
Unto their issue.

FOURTH PLEBEIAN

145 We'll hear the will. Read it, Mark Antony.

ALL

The will, the will! We will hear Caesar's will.

ANTONY

Have patience, gentle friends; I must not read it.
It is not meet you know how Caesar loved you.
You are not wood, you are not stones, but men;
150 And being men, hearing the will of Caesar,
It will inflame you, it will make you mad.
'Tis good you know not that you are his heirs,
For if you should, O what would come of it?

FOURTH PLEBEIAN

Read the will, we'll hear it, Antony.
155 You shall read us the will, Caesar's will.

ANTONY

Will you patient? Will you stay awhile?
I have o'ershot myself to tell you of it.
I fear I wrong the honorable men
Whose daggers have stabbed Caesar; I do fear it.

FOURTH PLEBEIAN

160 They were traitors. Honorable men!

ALL

The will! The testament!

to do wrong to the dead, to do wrong to myself and you,
rather than do wrong to such honorable men.
But here's a scroll with Caesar's seal on it.   135
I found it in his private room. It is his will.
If only the people could hear this testament
(which, pardon me, I don't intend to read),
they would go and kiss dead Caesar's wounds
and dip their handkerchiefs in his sacred blood;   140
indeed, they would beg to have one of his hairs to remember
    him by;
and when they died, they'd list that hair in their wills,
leaving it as a precious gift
to their children.

FOURTH CITIZEN
We want to hear the will. Read it, Mark Antony.   145

CITIZENS
The will, the will! We want to hear Caesar's will.

ANTONY
Be patient, noble friends. I must not read it.
It is not fitting for you to know how much Caesar loved you.
You aren't wood or stones, but men.
And because you are men, it would enrage you
to hear Caesar's will; it would drive you mad.   150
It is best for you not to know that you are his heirs—
for if you did, oh, what would come of it?

FOURTH CITIZEN
Read the will! We want to hear it, Antony.
You must read us the will—Caesar's will.   155

ANTONY
Will you be patient? Will you stay here while I read it?
I have gone too far in telling you about it.
I'm afraid I have done wrong to the honorable men
whose daggers have stabbed Caesar. I'm afraid of it.

FOURTH CITIZEN
They were traitors. Honorable men?   160

CITIZENS
The will! The testament!

SECOND PLEBEIAN

They were villains, murderers. The will! Read the will!

ANTONY

You will compel me then to read the will?
Then make a ring about the corpse of Caesar,
165 And let me show you him that made the will.
Shall I descend? And will you give me leave?

ALL

Come down.

SECOND PLEBEIAN

Descend.

THIRD PLEBEIAN

You shall have leave.

[ANTONY *descends.*]

FOURTH PLEBEIAN

170 A ring, stand round.

FIRST PLEBEIAN

Stand from the hearse, stand from the body.

SECOND PLEBEIAN

Room for Antony, most noble Antony.

ANTONY

Nay, press not so upon me; stand far off.

ALL

Stand back! Room! Bear back!

ANTONY

175 If you have tears, prepare to shed them now.
You all do know this mantle. I remember
The first time ever Caesar put it on;
'Twas on a summer's evening in his tent,
That day he overcame the Nervii.*
180 Look, in this place ran Cassius's dagger through.
See what a rent the envious Casca made.
Through this the well-beloved Brutus stabbed;
And as he plucked his cursed steel away,

---

179 *Nervii* a fierce tribe of Gaul conquered by Caesar in 57 B.C. at the battle of the Sambre, one of his most decisive victories

SECOND CITIZEN
They were villains and murderers! The will! Read the will.

ANTONY
So you demand that I read the will?
Then form a circle around Caesar's corpse,
and let me show you the man who wrote this will.   165
Should I come down? Do you give me permission to do so?

CITIZENS
Come down.

SECOND CITIZEN
Yes, come down.

THIRD CITIZEN
You have our permission.

      ANTONY *comes down from the platform.*

FOURTH CITIZEN
A circle; gather around Caesar.   170

FIRST CITIZEN
Leave space around the bier. Leave space around the body.

SECOND CITIZEN
Make room for Antony—most noble Antony.

ANTONY
No, don't crowd me like that. Stand farther away.

CITIZENS
Stand back! Make room! Move back!

ANTONY
If you have tears, get ready to shed them now.   175
You all recognize this cloak. I can remember
the first time Caesar ever put it on.
It was a summer evening in his tent—
the day he defeated the Nervii.
Look—here's the place where Cassius's dagger ran through.   180
And look at what a rip the spiteful Casca made.
Here's where Caesar's well-loved Brutus stabbed him;
and as Brutus pulled out his accursed blade,

Mark how the blood of Caesar followed it,
185 As rushing out of doors to be resolved
If Brutus so unkindly knocked, or no;
For Brutus, as you know, was Caesar's angel.
Judge, O you gods, how dearly Caesar loved him.
This was the most unkindest cut of all;
190 For when the noble Caesar saw him stab,
Ingratitude, more strong than traitor's arms,
Quite **vanquished** him. Then burst his mighty heart,
And in his mantle muffling up his face,
Even at the base of Pompey's statue,
195 Which all the while ran blood,* great Caesar fell.
O what a fall was there, my countrymen!
Then I, and you, and all of us fell down,
Whilst bloody treason flourished over us.
O now you weep, and I perceive you feel
200 The **dint** of pity. These are gracious drops.
Kind souls—what, weep you when you but behold
Our Caesar's vesture wounded? Look you here,

[ANTONY lifts Caesar's cloak.]

Here is himself, marred as you see with traitors.

FIRST PLEBEIAN
O piteous spectacle!

SECOND PLEBEIAN
205 O noble Caesar!

THIRD PLEBEIAN
O woeful day!

FOURTH PLEBEIAN
O traitors, villains!

FIRST PLEBEIAN
O most bloody sight!

SECOND PLEBEIAN
We will be revenged.

---

195 *ran blood* In popular belief, the corpse of a murdered man (here Pompey's
statue) bleeds in the presence of his murderer (Caesar). It seems more likely that
Antony means that Pompey's statue is bleeding in sympathetic outrage at the
murder of Caesar.

look at how Caesar's blood poured after it—
as if it were rushing outside to find out   185
whether or not it was Brutus knocking so rudely at the door.
For as you know, Caesar considered Brutus to be like an angel.
Oh, you gods, you know how dearly Caesar loved him!
This was the cruelest wound of all.
For when the noble Caesar saw Brutus stab him,   190
he was completely finished off by ingratitude,
which is stronger than traitors' weapons. Then his mighty heart
    burst,
and hiding his face with his cloak, great Caesar fell
right at the base of Pompey's statue,
which ran with blood the whole time.   195
Oh, what a fall that was, my countrymen!
Then you, and I, and all of us fell down,
while murderous treason swaggered over us.
Oh, now you are weeping—and I sense that you feel
the force of pity. These are generous teardrops.   200
Kind souls—what, do you weep when you only look
at Caesar's torn garment? Look here— (*He lifts off* CAESAR's *cloak.*)
Here is Caesar himself—mangled by the traitors, as you can see.

FIRST CITIZEN
Oh, what a pitiful spectacle!

SECOND CITIZEN
Oh, noble Caesar!   205

THIRD CITIZEN
Oh, what a sorrowful day!

FOURTH CITIZEN
Oh, the traitors, the villains!

FIRST CITIZEN
Oh, what a bloody sight!

SECOND PLEBEIAN
We'll get revenge.

ALL
210 Revenge! About! Seek! Burn! Fire! Kill! Slay!
Let not a traitor live!

ANTONY
Stay, countrymen.

FIRST PLEBEIAN
Peace there! Hear the noble Antony.

SECOND PLEBEIAN
We'll hear him, we'll follow him, we'll die with him.

ANTONY
215 Good friends, sweet friends, let me not stir you up
To such a sudden flood of mutiny.
They that have done this deed are honorable.
What private griefs they have, alas I know not,
That made them do it. They are wise and honorable,
220 And will no doubt with reasons answer you.
I come not, friends, to steal away your hearts;
I am no orator, as Brutus is,
But, as you know me all, a plain blunt man
That love my friend; and that they know full well
225 That gave me public leave to speak of him.
For I have neither wit, nor words, nor worth,
Action, nor utterance, nor the power of speech
To stir men's blood. I only speak right on.
I tell you that which you yourselves do know,
230 Show you sweet Caesar's wounds—poor poor dumb
mouths—
And bid them speak for me. But were I Brutus,
And Brutus Antony, there were an Antony
Would ruffle up your spirits, and put a tongue
235 In every wound of Caesar, that should move
The stones of Rome to rise and mutiny.

ALL
We'll mutiny.

FIRST PLEBEIAN
We'll burn the house of Brutus.

THIRD PLEBEIAN
Away, then; come, seek the conspirators.

CITIZENS
Revenge! Let's go! Look for them! Burn them! Set fires!
Kill them! Slay them! Don't let a single traitor live!

ANTONY
Wait, countrymen.

FIRST CITIZEN
Quiet, there! Listen to the noble Antony.

SECOND CITIZEN
We'll listen to him, we'll follow him, and we'll die with him.

ANTONY
Good friends, sweet friends, don't let me stir you up   215
to such a sudden outburst of rebellion.
The men who did this deed are honorable.
Alas, I don't know what personal grievances
made them kill Caesar. But they are wise and honorable,
and I'm sure they'll answer you with good reasons.   220
Friends, I have not come to steal your loyalty.
I'm not an orator, like Brutus is;
instead, you all know me as a plain, blunt man
who loved his friend—and the men who gave me permission
to speak in public about him also know me to be such a man.   225
For I have no cleverness, learned words, personal authority,
skillful gestures, or delivery, or an impressive voice
to stir men's blood; I can only speak directly.
So I tell you what you already know yourselves,
and show you sweet Caesar's wounds—these poor, silent   230
   mouths—
and ask them to speak for me. But if I were Brutus,
and if Brutus were Antony, there would be an Antony
who could enrage your spirits and make
every one of Caesar's wounds speak so they could stir up   235
even the stones of Rome to rise in rebellion.

CITIZENS
We'll rebel.

FIRST CITIZEN
We'll burn down Brutus's house.

THIRD CITIZEN
Let's go, then. Come on, let's find the conspirators.

ANTONY

240   Yet hear me, countrymen; yet hear me speak.

ALL

Peace, ho! Hear Antony, most noble Antony.

ANTONY

Why, friends, you go to do you know not what.
Wherein hath Caesar thus deserved your loves?
Alas, you know not; I must tell you then.
245   You have forgot the will I told you of.

ALL

Most true, the will; let's stay and hear the will.

ANTONY

Here is the will, and under Caesar's seal.
To every Roman citizen he gives,
To every several man, seventy-five drachmas.*

SECOND PLEBEIANS

250   Most noble Caesar, we'll revenge his death.

THIRD PLEBEIAN

O royal Caesar!

ANTONY

Hear me with patience.

ALL

Peace, ho!

ANTONY

Moreover, he hath left you all his walks,
255   His private arbors, and new-planted orchards,
On this side Tiber; he hath left them you,
And to your heirs forever: common pleasures,
To walk abroad and recreate yourselves.
Here was a Caesar! When comes such another?

FIRST PLEBEIAN

260   Never, never.—Come, away, away!
We'll burn his body in the holy place,

---

249   *seventy-five drachmas*   The drachma was an ancient Greek silver coin.

ANTONY
But listen to me, countrymen; listen to me speak. 240

CITIZENS
Quiet, everyone! Listen to Antony—most noble Antony!

ANTONY
Why, friends—you don't even know what you're about to do.
Why does Caesar deserve for you to love him so?
Alas, you don't know. I must tell you, then.
You've forgotten the will I told you about. 245

CITIZENS
That's true. The will! Let's wait and hear the will.

ANTONY
Here is the will, with Caesar's seal on it.
To every Roman—to each individual man—
he gives seventy-five drachmas.

SECOND CITIZEN
Most noble Caesar! We'll avenge his death. 250

THIRD CITIZEN
Oh, generous Caesar!

ANTONY
Listen to me patiently.

CITIZENS
Listen, everyone!

ANTONY
He has also left you all his walking paths,
his private woods, and his newly planted gardens 255
on this side of the river Tiber. He has left them to you
and your descendants forever—public parks
where you can take walks and enjoy yourselves.
This is what Caesar was like! When will there be another like him?

FIRST CITIZEN
Never, never!—Come on, let's go, let's go! 260
We'll burn his body in the holy place,

And with the brands fire the traitors' houses.
Take up the body.

SECOND PLEBEIAN
Go fetch fire.

THIRD PLEBEIAN
265   Pluck down benches.

FOURTH PLEBEIAN
Pluck down forms, windows, anything.

Exit PLEBEIANS [*with* CAESAR'S *body*].

ANTONY
Now let it work. Mischief, thou art afoot,
Take thou what course thou wilt.

Enter SERVANT.

How now, fellow?

SERVANT
270   Sir, Octavius is already come to Rome.

ANTONY
Where is he?

SERVANT
He and Lepidus* are at Caesar's home.

ANTONY
And thither will I straight to visit him.
He comes upon a wish. Fortune is merry,
275   And in this mood will give us anything.

SERVANT
I heard him say Brutus and Cassius
Are rid like madmen through the gates of Rome.

ANTONY
Belike they had some notice of the people
How I had moved them. Bring me to Octavius.

Exeunt.

---

272   *Lepidus* Marcus Aemilius Lepidus, a supporter of Caesar and consul with him in
46 B.C., was outside Rome with an army at the time of Caesar's assassination. He
later became one of the Triumvirate with Antony and Octavius.

then set fire to the traitors' houses with the burning coals.
Pick up the body.

SECOND CITIZEN
Go get some fire.

THIRD CITIZEN
Tear loose some benches. 265

FOURTH CITIZEN
Tear loose benches, window shutters, anything.

The CITIZENS exit with CAESAR'S body.

ANTONY
Now let matters work themselves out. Mischief, you're on the
    loose;
take whatever actions you like.

The SERVANT enters.

What is it, fellow?

SERVANT
Sir, Octavius has already arrived in Rome. 270

ANTONY
Where is he?

SERVANT
He and Lepidus are at Caesar's house.

ANTONY
And I will go there right away to visit him.
He has arrived just when I hoped he would. Fortune is smiling—
and in this mood, she will give us anything. 275

SERVANT
I heard him say that Brutus and Cassius
have ridden like madmen out of the gates of Rome.

ANTONY
They probably heard news about the people
and how I stirred them up. Take me to Octavius.

They exit.

ACT III, SCENE III

[Rome. A street.] Enter CINNA *the poet, and after him the* PLEBEIANS.

CINNA

I dreamt tonight that I did feast with Caesar,
And things unluckily charge my fantasy.
I have no will to wander forth of doors,
Yet something leads me forth.

FIRST PLEBEIAN

5   What is your name?

SECOND PLEBEIAN

Whither are you going?

THIRD PLEBEIAN

Where do you dwell?

FOURTH PLEBEIAN

Are you a married man or a bachelor?

SECOND PLEBEIAN

Answer every man directly.

FIRST PLEBEIAN

10   Ay, and briefly.

FOURTH PLEBEIAN

Ay, and wisely.

THIRD PLEBEIAN

Ay, and truly, you were best.

CINNA

What is my name? Whither am I going? Where do I dwell?
Am I a married man or a bachelor? Then, to answer every
15   man directly and briefly, wisely and truly: wisely I say, I
am a bachelor.

SECOND PLEBEIAN

That's as much as to say, they are fools that marry. You'll
bear me a bang for that, I fear. Proceed directly.

CINNA

Directly I am going to Caesar's funeral.

ACT 3, SCENE 3

A street. CINNA *the poet enters, followed by* CITIZENS.

CINNA
Last night, I dreamed that I feasted with Caesar—
and now everything that happens seems ominous to me.
I had no desire to go out of doors,
yet something prompted me to go outside.

FIRST CITIZEN
What is your name? 5

SECOND CITIZEN
Where are you going?

THIRD CITIZEN
Where do you live?

FOURTH CITIZEN
Are you a married man or a bachelor?

SECOND CITIZEN
Answer each of us straightforwardly.

FIRST CITIZEN
Yes, and briefly. 10

FOURTH CITIZEN
Yes, and wisely.

THIRD CITIZEN
Yes, and honestly, too, if you know what's good for you.

CINNA
What is my name? Where am I going? Where do I live? Am I a
married man or a bachelor? I'll answer each of you straight- 15
forwardly, briefly, wisely, and honestly. I tell you, wisely,
I am a bachelor.

SECOND CITIZEN
You're as much as saying that those who marry are fools. You'll
get a blow from me for that, I'm afraid. Continue, straightforwardly.

CINNA
Straightforwardly, I am going to Caesar's funeral.

FIRST PLEBEIAN

20   As a friend or an enemy?

CINNA

As a friend.

SECOND PLEBEIAN

The matter is answered directly.

FOURTH PLEBEIAN

For your dwelling—briefly.

CINNA

Briefly, I dwell by the Capitol.

THIRD PLEBEIAN

25   Your name, sir, truly.

CINNA

Truly, my name is Cinna.

FIRST PLEBEIAN

Tear him to pieces, he's a conspirator.

CINNA

I am Cinna the poet, I am Cinna the poet.

FOURTH PLEBEIAN

Tear him for his bad verses, tear him for his bad verses.

CINNA

30   I am not Cinna the conspirator.

FOURTH PLEBEIAN

It is no matter, his name's Cinna; pluck but his name out
of his heart and turn him going.

THIRD PLEBEIAN

Tear him, tear him! Come, brands, ho, firebrands! To
Brutus's, to Cassius's, burn all! Some to Decius's house
35   and some to Casca's; some to Ligarius's. Away, go!

Exeunt all the PLEBEIANS [*with* CINNA].

FIRST CITIZEN
As a friend or an enemy? 20

CINNA
As a friend.

SECOND CITIZEN
He answered that question straightforwardly.

FOURTH CITIZEN
Tell us where you live—briefly.

CINNA
Briefly, I live near the Capitol.

THIRD CITIZEN
Tell us your name, sir—honestly. 25

CINNA
Honestly, my name is Cinna.

FIRST CITIZEN
Tear him to pieces! He's a conspirator.

CINNA
I am Cinna the poet, I am Cinna the poet!

FOURTH CITIZEN
Tear him apart because of his bad poems, tear him apart
because of his bad poems!

CINNA
I am not Cinna the conspirator. 30

FOURTH CITIZEN
It doesn't matter. His name is Cinna. Rip his name out of his
heart, then finish him off.

THIRD CITIZEN
Tear him apart, tear him apart! Come on, bring some hot
coals—some burning sticks! Let's go to Brutus's house, to
Cassius's house, and burn them all. Some go to Decius's house,
some to Casca's, some to Ligarius's. Come on, let's go! 35

All the CITIZENS *exit, carrying off* CINNA.

Act III Review

Discussion Questions

1. What is the dramatic effect of the opening dialogue in Scene i?

2. What is the final image of Caesar?

3. What change do we see in Antony during his soliloquy over Caesar's corpse (Scene i, lines 274–295)?

4. Why does Brutus's speech in Scene ii ultimately fail?

5. Caesar's last words are "*Et tu, Bruté*?—Then fall, Caesar." What do Caesar's words mean? Explain why you think Caesar reacts this way when he sees Brutus with the murderers.

6. Antony's speech turns the crowd against the conspirators. But what might have happened if Brutus and Cassius had refused to let Antony speak to the crowd? Think about some possible outcomes, and be ready to discuss them with the class.

7. Cinna the poet is murdered on the street by the mob even though he is not Lucius Cornelius Cinna, the conspirator. Do you think a single citizen would have attacked Cinna as opposed to a mob? Explain why or why not.

8. After Caesar's murder, what kind of leader does Rome most desperately need? Decide which of the two funeral orators—Brutus or Antony—is the better leader and explain your opinion.

Literary Elements

1. In Scene i, Antony predicts that Caesar's death will **cause** terrible things to happen. Look at lines 279–295 and note what **effects** he foresees as a result of Caesar's assassination.

2. An **inference** is a judgment the reader can make based on clues in a text. Look at the passages in Act III, Scene i where Antony speaks to the conspirators after learning of Caesar's death. From Antony's words and thoughts, what can you infer about his real feelings regarding Caesar's murder?

3. **Rhetoric** is effective communication in writing or in speech. Compare the speeches of Brutus and Antony at Caesar's funeral and decide what makes one of them more effective than the other. Look for persuasive techniques such as **repetition**, strong **imagery**, **rhythm**, **diction** (word choice), and **emotional appeals**, in addition to others. Which speaker do the Roman crowds find more believable?

4. **Repetition** can be an effective technique for increasing the tension and emotional impact of a speech or scene. Reread Scene iii, in which Cinna is questioned by the crowd. What is the effect of the repetition in this scene?

Writing Prompts

1. Write a description of Brutus or Antony based on what you have learned about him so far. Use specific quotes from the play to support your writing.

2. In Scene ii, Cassius goes off to give his own speech about the reasons for killing Caesar. Write his speech, based on what you have learned about him in the play.

3. Look back at your answer to #2 in the Literary Elements. Why do you think the crowd of Romans responded emotionally to Antony's speech and not to Brutus's? Write a short essay explaining the effectiveness of Antony's funeral oration.

4. In real life, the common people of Rome rioted for three days after the burial of Caesar. As a human interest story to accompany the news report of Caesar's death, "interview" various citizens from Rome, and report on the mood of the city.

Julius Caesar

Act IV

Dennis Boulsikaris, as Cassius, and Jamey Sheridan, as Brutus, Shakespeare in Central Park , 2000

"There is a tide in the affairs of men,
which, taken at the flood, leads
on to fortune; omitted, all the
voyage of their life is bound
in shallows and in miseries."

⊕ ⊕ ⊕

Before You Read

1. What is your opinion of Antony at this point in the play? Think about what part you expect him to play in future events.

2. Do you think that Brutus is "an honorable man"? Explain why or why not.

3. What do you expect to become of the conspirators and their hopes?

Literary Elements

1. A **tragedy** is a serious work of literature that narrates the events leading to the downfall of a **tragic hero**, who in almost every way displays noble qualities. This person's downfall is a result of a **tragic flaw** or fatal character weakness. In *Julius Caesar*, for example, the title character is a tragic hero whose fatal flaw is blind ambition.

2. Conversation between characters is **dialogue**. Good dialogue moves the plot forward and conveys clues about the characters' motivations and feelings. In Act II, Scene i of *Julius Caesar*, Portia begged Brutus to tell her what was troubling him in a dialogue filled with love and signs of mutual respect.

3. **Imagery** is highly descriptive language that appeals to one or more of the five senses—touch, taste, hearing, smell, and sight. In Act III, Brutus used powerful imagery to urge the Roman senators to celebrate their liberation from Caesar's tyranny. "Stoop, Romans, stoop / And let us bathe our hands in Caesar's blood / Up to the elbows and besmear our swords."

4. A **metaphor** is a figure of speech that makes a comparison between things that are not truly alike. An **extended metaphor** is a complex comparison that goes on for several lines, comparing the unlike things point by point. In Act I, Scene i, lines 71–74, Caesar is likened to a bird and his followers to feathers.

Words to Know

The following vocabulary words appear in Act IV in the original text of Shakespeare's play. However, they are words that are still commonly used. Read the definitions here and pay attention to the words as you read the play (they will be in boldfaced type).

base	low; dishonorable
chastisement	punishment; scolding
corporal	bodily; physical
covert	hidden; concealed
disclosed	revealed; made known
legacies	gifts by will; bequests
mettle	courage; strength of character
proscription	ban; prohibition
salutation	expression of greeting or goodwill
slanderous [sland'rous]	insulting; false

Act Summary

Several months after coming to power, the Second Triumvirate—Antony, Octavius, and Lepidus—is meeting to agree on a list of enemies. In order to strengthen their authority, they must eliminate anyone who might oppose them.

They learn that Brutus and Cassius are mobilizing to confront them and revive the ideals of the old Roman Republic.

In Brutus's tent at Sardis, he and Cassius have a heated exchange. Brutus complains that Cassius is dishonoring their party by raising funds with "base bribes." Cassius denies the charge, baring his breast to Brutus and urging him to strike Cassius as he did Caesar.

Brutus admits that his foul mood is influenced by the suicide of his wife, Portia. Messala arrives and tells them that their enemies Octavius and Antony are moving toward Philippi with an enormous army. The would-be dictators have carried out their plan to ruin the Senate by murdering one hundred senators, including the eminent Cicero, Brutus's friend.

Cassius and Brutus argue briefly about their military strategy, with Brutus insisting they meet the enemy on the field at Philippi in open battle. Later, while others sleep and Brutus reads, he is visited by the ghost of Caesar. Caesar's ghost warns him that the two will meet again at Philippi.

Brutus sees Julius Caesar's ghost, 1892 playbill

ACT IV, SCENE I

[*Rome. Antony's house.*] *Enter* ANTONY, OCTAVIUS, *and* LEPIDUS.

ANTONY
These many then shall die; their names are pricked.

OCTAVIUS
Your brother too must die. Consent you, Lepidus?

LEPIDUS
I do consent—

OCTAVIUS
                Prick him down, Antony.

LEPIDUS
5   Upon condition Publius shall not live,
Who is your sister's son, Mark Antony.

ANTONY
He shall not live. Look, with a spot I damn him.
But, Lepidus, go you to Caesar's house.
Fetch the will hither, and we shall determine
10   How to cut off some charge in **legacies**.

LEPIDUS
What, shall I find you here?

OCTAVIUS
Or here, or at the Capitol.

    Exit LEPIDUS.

ANTONY
This is a slight unmeritable man,
Meet to be sent on errands. Is it fit,
15   The threefold world* divided, he should stand
One of the three to share it?

---

15   *threefold world*   When the Triumvirate was established in 43 B.C., Antony,
Octavius, and Lepidus each laid claim to a different sphere of influence in the
Roman Empire (extending over Europe, Africa, and Asia).

ACT 4, SCENE 1

A house in Rome. ANTONY, OCTAVIUS, *and* LEPIDUS *enter.*

ANTONY
So these many men will die; their names are checked off.

OCTAVIUS
Your brother must die, too, Lepidus. Do you agree?

LEPIDUS
I agree—

OCTAVIUS
Mark him off, Antony.

LEPIDUS
—but only on the condition that Publius not live;   5
and he's your sister's son, Mark Antony.

ANTONY
He won't live. Look, I condemn him with a mark.
Now, Lepidus, go to Caesar's house.
bring his will from there, and we shall see
if we can cut down on some of the bequests.   10

LEPIDUS
Will I still find you here?

OCTAVIUS
Here or else at the Capitol.

     LEPIDUS *exits.*

ANTONY
This is a worthless, undeserving man,
fit to be sent on errands. Is it proper
that he should be one of the three men to share   15
a world divided up three ways?

OCTAVIUS

So you thought him,
And took his voice who should be pricked to die
In our black sentence and proscription.

ANTONY

20 Octavius, I have seen more days than you;
And though we lay these honors on this man
To ease ourselves of divers **sland'rous** loads,
He shall but bear them as the ass bears gold,
To groan and sweat under the business,
25 Either led or driven as we point the way;
And having brought our treasure where we will,
Then take we down his load and turn him off,
Like to the empty ass, to shake his ears
And graze in commons.

OCTAVIUS

30 You may do your will;
But he's a tried and valiant soldier.

ANTONY

So is my horse, Octavius, and for that
I do appoint him store of provender.
It is a creature that I teach to fight,
35 To wind, to stop, to run directly on,
His **corporal** motion governed by my spirit.
And, in some taste, is Lepidus but so.
He must be taught, and trained, and bid go forth:
A barren-spirited fellow; one that feeds
40 On objects, arts, and imitations,
Which, out of use and staled by other men,
Begin his fashion. Do not talk of him
But as a property. And now, Octavius,
Listen great things. Brutus and Cassius
45 Are levying powers. We must straight make head.
Therefore let our alliance be combined,
Our best friends made, our means stretched;
And let us presently go sit in council

OCTAVIUS

You thought him fit
and accepted his opinions as to who should be marked to die
in our sentences of death and exile.

ANTONY

Octavius, I am older and more experienced than you;   20
and although we pile honors on this man
to shift some of our burden of blame onto him,
he will carry those honors just like a donkey carries gold;
he'll groan and sweat at his heavy work,
whether he's led or driven, while we point the way;   25
and when he's taken our treasure where we want it to go,
then we will take off his load and turn him loose,
like an unloaded ass, to shake his ears
and graze in the public pasture.

OCTAVIUS

You may do as you like,   30
but he's an experienced and brave soldier.

ANTONY

So is my horse, Octavius—and for that,
I give him a good supply of feed.
He is a creature that I teach to fight,
to turn, to stop, to run straight ahead—   35
his physical movements always ruled by my mind.
And to some degree, Lepidus is no more than that.
He must be taught, trained, and commanded to go forth.
He's a fellow without initiative, who takes up
novelties, styles, and fads   40
that have grown stale and out-of-date to everyone else,
and thinks they are the height of fashion. Don't speak of him
as anything but a means to an end. And now, Octavius,
listen to important things. Brutus and Cassius
are raising armies. We must press forward immediately.   45
And so let's bring together our alliance,
summon our best friends, and make the most of our means;
and let us immediately hold a meeting

How **covert** matters may be best **disclosed**,
50 And open perils surest answered.

OCTAVIUS
Let us do so, for we are at the stake*
And bayed about with many enemies,
And some that smile have in their hearts, I fear,
Millions of mischiefs.

Exeunt.

---

51 *at the stake*   an image from the Elizabethan sport of bearbaiting, in which a bear
was chained to a stake in the middle of an arena and then attacked by dogs

to decide how we can best discover hidden dangers
and safely respond to dangers that are out in the open.   50

OCTAVIUS
Let us do so, for we are tied to a stake
and surrounded by many enemies,
and I'm afraid that some of them who smile
actually have millions of plans in their hearts to harm us.

They exit.

ACT IV, SCENE II

[The camp near Sardis*; before the tent of Brutus.]
Drum. Enter BRUTUS, LUCILIUS, [LUCIUS,] and the
ARMY. TITINIUS and PINDARUS meet them.

BRUTUS

Stand, ho!

LUCILIUS

Give the word, ho! And stand!

BRUTUS

What now, Lucilius, is Cassius near?

LUCILIUS

He is at hand, and Pindarus is come

5   To do you **salutation** from his master.

BRUTUS

He greets me well. Your master, Pindarus,
In his own change, or by ill officers,
Hath given me some worthy cause to wish
Things done undone; but if he be at hand,

10   I shall be satisfied.

PINDARUS

I do not doubt
But that my noble master will appear
Such as he is, full of regard and honor.

BRUTUS

He is not doubted.

[BRUTUS and LUCILIUS walk aside.]

A word, Lucilius,

15   How he received you. Let me be resolved.

LUCILIUS

With courtesy and with respect enough,
But not with such familiar instances,

Sardis   capital of Lydia, a kingdom in western Asia Minor, now part of western Turkey

ACT 4, SCENE 2

Camp near Sardis. Drums. BRUTUS, LUCILIUS, LUCIUS, *and the* ARMY *enter.* TITINIUS *and* PINDARUS *meet them.*

BRUTUS
Halt!

LUCILIUS
Give the command to halt!

BRUTUS
Tell me, Lucilius—is Cassius approaching?

LUCILIUS
He has arrived, and Pindarus has come
to bring greetings from his master.   5

BRUTUS
Cassius sends his greetings by a good man.—Pindarus,
either because of some change in his feelings toward me, or
    because of the actions of bad subordinates,
your master has given me good reason to wish
some things which have been done were undone; but if he has
    arrived,
I'll get a satisfactory explanation.   10

PINDARUS
I am sure
that my noble master will show himself
to be what he is—worthy of your respect and honor.

BRUTUS
I don't doubt that about him.

        BRUTUS *and* LUCILIUS *walk aside.*

Tell me
how he greeted you, Lucilius. Inform me fully.   15

LUCILIUS
He greeted me with enough courtesy and respect—
but not with the same displays of friendship

Nor with such free and friendly conference
As he hath used of old.

BRUTUS

20   Thou hast described
A hot friend cooling. Ever note, Lucilius,
When love begins to sicken and decay
It useth an enforced ceremony.
There are no tricks in plain and simple faith;
25   But hollow men, like horses hot at hand,
Make gallant show and promise of their **mettle**;

      Low march within.

But when they should endure the bloody spur,
They fall their crests, and, like deceitful jades,
Sink in the trial. Comes his army on?

LUCILIUS

30   They mean this night in Sardis to be quartered.
The greater part, the horse in general,
Are come with Cassius.

      Enter CASSIUS *and his* POWERS.

BRUTUS

                           Hark, he is arrived.
March gently on to meet him.

CASSIUS

35   Stand, ho!

BRUTUS

Stand, ho! Speak the word along.

[FIRST SOLDIER]

Stand!

[SECOND SOLDIER]

Stand!

[THIRD SOLDIER]

Stand!

CASSIUS

40   Most noble brother,* you have done me wrong.

---

40   *brother*   literally, brother-in-law, although Cassius may also mean it in the wider
sense of "dear friend"

190   *Julius Caesar*

or open and friendly conversation
as he used to engage in.

BRUTUS
You've just described 20
a warm friend cooling off. Always observe, Lucilius,
how when a friend begins to grow more distant,
he puts on forced politeness.
There are no pretenses in a plain and simple friendship;
but insincere men, like horses which seem fiery at first, 25
act brave and promise to be courageous;

Marching is heard offstage.

but when they're actually spurred by their riders,
they let their necks drop, and like dishonest nags,
they fail at the test. Is his army approaching?

LUCILIUS
They plan to quarter themselves tonight in Sardis. 30
Most of the army, and all of the cavalry,
have come with Cassius.

CASSIUS and his ARMY enter.

BRUTUS
Look, he has arrived.
March slowly to meet him.

CASSIUS
Halt! 35

BRUTUS
Halt! Pass the command along.

FIRST SOLDIER
Halt!

SECOND SOLDIER
Halt!

THIRD SOLDIER
Halt!

CASSIUS
Most noble brother, you have done me wrong.

BRUTUS

Judge me, you gods! Wrong I mine enemies?
And if not so, how should I wrong a brother?

CASSIUS

Brutus, this sober form of yours hides wrongs,
And when you do them—

BRUTUS

45   Cassius, be content.
Speak your griefs softly; I do know you well.
Before the eyes of both our armies here,
Which should perceive nothing but love from us,
Let us not wrangle. Bid them move away;
50   Then in my tent, Cassius, enlarge your griefs,
And I will give you audience.

CASSIUS

                  Pindarus,
Bid our commanders lead their charges off
A little from this ground.

BRUTUS

55   Lucius, do you the like; and let no man
Come to our tent till we have done our conference.
Let Lucilius and Titinius guard our door.

      Exeunt.

BRUTUS

Be my judge, you gods! Have I ever done wrong even to my
enemies?
If not, how could I ever do wrong to a brother?

CASSIUS

Brutus, this dignified manner of yours covers up your wrongs,
and when you do them—

BRUTUS

Cassius, calm down.   45
Speak of your grievances more quietly. I understand you well.
Both of our armies are here,
and they should see nothing but love between us,
so let's not quarrel. Command them to move away.
Then tell me your grievances inside my tent,   50
where I will listen to you.

CASSIUS

Pindarus,
command our officers to lead their troops
a little way from here.

BRUTUS

Lucius, do the same, and make sure that no one   55
comes into our tent until we've finished talking.
Let Lucilius and Titinius guard our door.

All but BRUTUS *and* CASSIUS *exit.*

ACT IV, SCENE III

[*The camp near Sardis; within the tent of Brutus.*]
BRUTUS *and* CASSIUS *remain.*

CASSIUS

That you have wronged me doth appear in this:
You have condemned and noted Lucius Pella
For taking bribes here of the Sardians;
Wherein my letters, praying on his side,
5   Because I knew the man, was slighted off.

BRUTUS

You wronged yourself to write in such a case.

CASSIUS

In such a time as this it is not meet
That every nice offense should bear his comment.

BRUTUS

Let me tell you, Cassius, you yourself
10   Are much condemned to have an itching palm,
To sell and mart your offices for gold
To undeservers.

CASSIUS

                    I, an itching palm?
You know that you are Brutus that speaks this,
15   Or, by the gods, this speech were else your last.

BRUTUS

The name of Cassius honors this corruption,
And **chastisement** doth therefore hide his head.

CASSIUS

Chastisement?

BRUTUS

Remember March; the ides of March remember.
20   Did not great Julius bleed for justice's sake?
What villain touched his body that did stab,
And not for justice? What, shall one of us,
That struck the foremost man of all this world

ACT 4, SCENE 3

The camp near Sardis. Brutus's tent. BRUTUS *and* CASSIUS *remain.*

CASSIUS
Here's why it is obvious that you have wronged me:
You condemned and publicly disgraced Lucius Pella
for taking bribes from the Sardians here,
and you scornfully disregarded my letters
in which I pled on his behalf because I knew him.   5

BRUTUS
You did yourself wrong by writing on his behalf.

CASSIUS
At a time like now, it's not proper
for every trivial fault to be criticized.

BRUTUS
Let me tell you, Cassius, that you yourself
have been accused of having a greedy streak,   10
and of selling and marketing high positions to unworthy people
for gold.

CASSIUS
I, a greedy streak?
If you were anyone but Brutus and said this,
you know that these words would be your last.   15

BRUTUS
The name of Cassius makes this kind of corruption seem
    respectable,
and so punishment is never carried out.

CASSIUS
Punishment?

BRUTUS
Remember March; remember March 15.
Didn't great Julius die for the sake of justice?   20
Were any of us so villainous that we stabbed him
for any reason except justice? Should those of us
who killed the most powerful man in all the world,

But for supporting robbers, shall we now
25 Contaminate our fingers with **base** bribes,
And sell the mighty space of our large honors
For so much trash as may be grasped thus?
I had rather be a dog, and bay the moon,
Than such a Roman.

CASSIUS

30   Brutus, bait not me,
I'll not endure it. You forget yourself
To hedge me in. I am a soldier, I,
Older in practice, abler than yourself
To make conditions.

BRUTUS

35   Go to! You are not, Cassius.

CASSIUS

I am.

BRUTUS

I say you are not.

CASSIUS

Urge me no more, I shall forget myself.
Have mind upon your health. Tempt me no farther.

BRUTUS

40 Away, slight man!

CASSIUS

Is 't possible?

BRUTUS

                        Hear me, for I will speak.
Must I give way and room to your rash choler?
Shall I be frighted when a madman stares?

CASSIUS

45 O ye gods, ye gods! Must I endure all this?

BRUTUS

All this? Ay, more. Fret till your proud heart break.
Go show your slaves how choleric you are,
And make your bondmen tremble. Must I budge?
Must I observe you? Must I stand and crouch

only because he tolerated corrupt officials,
now pollute our fingers with filthy bribes,   25
selling our vast power to grant honors and positions
for the kind of money that can be held in one's hand?
I'd rather be a dog that howled at the moon
than such a Roman.

CASSIUS

Brutus, don't harass me.   30
I won't put up with it. You forget who you are
when you try to limit my powers. I am a soldier,
more experienced than you are and better able
to manage practical matters.

BRUTUS

Nonsense! You are not, Cassius.   35

CASSIUS

I am.

BRUTUS

I say that you are not.

CASSIUS

Don't push me any more. I'll lose control of myself.
Show some concern for your own safety. Don't goad me further.

BRUTUS

Get out of here, you insignificant man!   40

CASSIUS

Is this possible?

BRUTUS

Listen, I've got something to tell you.
Should I step back and make room for your reckless anger?
Should I be scared just because a madman glares at me?

CASSIUS

Oh, you gods, you gods! Must I put up with all this?   45

BRUTUS

All this? Yes, and more. Rant until your proud heart breaks.
Go show your slaves how easily enraged you are,
and make your servants tremble with fear. Must I cower at this
    outburst?
Must I show you cringing respect? Must I stand or bow

50   Under your testy humor? By the gods,
      You shall digest the venom of your spleen
      Though it do split you. For, from this day forth,
      I'll use you for my mirth, yea, for my laughter,
      When you are waspish.

CASSIUS

55   Is it come to this?

BRUTUS
      You say you are a better soldier.
      Let it appear so; make your vaunting true,
      And it shall please me well. For mine own part,
      I shall be glad to learn of noble men.

CASSIUS

60   You wrong me every way; you wrong me, Brutus.
      I said an elder soldier, not a better.
      Did I say "better"?

BRUTUS

                         If you did, I care not.

CASSIUS
      When Caesar lived, he durst not thus have moved me.

BRUTUS

65   Peace, peace! You durst not so have tempted him.

CASSIUS
      I durst not?

BRUTUS
      No.

CASSIUS
      What, durst not tempt him?

BRUTUS

                              For your life you durst not.

CASSIUS

70   Do not presume too much upon my love;
      I may do that I shall be sorry for.

BRUTUS
      You have done that you should be sorry for.
      There is no terror, Cassius, in your threats;

according to your changeable mood? By the gods,   50
you'll have to swallow the poison of your fierce temper
even if it splits you in half. For from this day on,
I'll use you for my merriment—indeed, for my laughter—
whenever you are irritable.

CASSIUS

Have things come to this?   55

BRUTUS

You say that you're a better soldier.
Show me it's so, prove that your boasting is true,
and it will please me well. As for me,
I'm glad to learn lessons from noble men.

CASSIUS

You do me wrong in every way; you do me wrong, Brutus.   60
I said a more experienced soldier, not a better one.
Did I say "better"?

BRUTUS

I don't care if you did.

CASSIUS

When Caesar lived, he wouldn't have dared anger me like this.

BRUTUS

Hush, hush! You wouldn't have dared provoke him.   65

CASSIUS

I wouldn't have dared?

BRUTUS

No.

CASSIUS

What—wouldn't have dared provoke him?

BRUTUS

Not even to save your life.

CASSIUS

Don't take my affection for you too much for granted.   70
I may do something I'll be sorry for.

BRUTUS

You've already done things you should be sorry for.
Cassius, I feel no terror because of your threats,

For I am armed so strong in honesty
75 That they pass by me as the idle wind,
Which I respect not. I did send to you
For certain sums of gold, which you denied me,
For I can raise no money by vile means.
By heaven, I had rather coin my heart,
80 And drop my blood for drachmas than to wring
From the hard hands of peasants their vile trash
By any indirection. I did send
To you for gold to pay my legions,
Which you denied me. Was that done like Cassius?
85 Should I have answered Caius Cassius so?
When Marcus Brutus grows so covetous
To lock such rascal counters from his friends,
Be ready, gods, with all your thunderbolts;
Dash him to pieces.

CASSIUS

90   I denied you not.

BRUTUS

You did.

CASSIUS

I did not. He was but a fool
That brought my answer back. Brutus hath rived my heart.
A friend should bear his friend's infirmities,
95 But Brutus makes mine greater than they are.

BRUTUS

I do not, till you practice them on me.

CASSIUS

You love me not.

BRUTUS

                    I do not like your faults.

CASSIUS

A friendly eye could never see such faults.

BRUTUS

100 A flatterer's would not, though they do appear
As huge as high Olympus.

for I am so strongly armored by my own integrity
that your threats pass by me like a slight breeze   75
which I ignore. I sent a message to you
asking for a certain amount of gold, which you refused to give me,
for I can't raise money by dishonest means.
By heaven, I'd rather turn my heart into coins
and shed my own blood for money than to wring   80
from the calloused hands of peasants their miserable cash
by any deceitful means. I sent a message to you,
asking you for gold to pay my troops,
and you refused. Was it like Cassius to do that?
Would I have answered Caius Cassius like that?   85
When Marcus Brutus becomes so greedy
that he locks up worthless coins from his friends,
be ready, gods, with all your thunderbolts:
blast him to pieces!

CASSIUS
I didn't refuse you.   90

BRUTUS
You did.

CASSIUS
I didn't. The man who brought my answer to you
got the message wrong. Brutus has broken my heart.
A friend should put up with his friend's weaknesses,
but Brutus makes mine seem worse than they are.   95

BRUTUS
I didn't until you started turning your weaknesses against me.

CASSIUS
You don't love me.

BRUTUS
I don't like your faults.

CASSIUS
The eye of a friend would never see such faults.

BRUTUS
The eye of a flatterer wouldn't see them, even if they   100
were as huge as Mt. Olympus.

CASSIUS

    Come, Antony, and young Octavius, come!
    Revenge yourselves alone on Cassius,
    For Cassius is aweary of the world;
105   Hated by one he loves, braved by his brother,
    Checked like a bondman, all his faults observed,
    Set in a notebook, learned, and conned by rote
    To cast into my teeth. O I could weep
    My spirit from mine eyes! There is my dagger,
110   And here my naked breast; within, a heart
    Dearer than Pluto's mine,* richer than gold.
    If that thou be'st a Roman, take it forth.
    I that denied thee gold will give my heart.
    Strike as thou didst at Caesar; for I know,
115   When thou didst hate him worst, thou lovedst him better
    Than ever thou lovedst Cassius.

BRUTUS

                        Sheathe your dagger.
    Be angry when you will, it shall have scope.
    Do what you will, dishonor shall be humor.
120   O Cassius, you are yoked with a lamb,
    That carries anger as the flint bears fire;
    Who, much enforced, shows a hasty spark
    And straight is cold again.

CASSIUS

                      Hath Cassius lived
125   To be but mirth and laughter to his Brutus,
    When grief and blood ill-tempered* vexeth him?

BRUTUS

    When I spoke that, I was ill-tempered too.

CASSIUS

    Do you confess so much? Give me your hand.

---

111 *Pluto's mine* Pluto, god of the underworld, rules over all the riches in mines,
although there was a common confusion between Pluto and Plutus, the god of
wealth.

CASSIUS

Come on, Antony and young Octavius! Come on!
Take revenge on Cassius and no one else,
for Cassius is weary of the world;
he's hated by someone he loves, threatened by his brother,   105
scolded like a slave. All my faults have been studied,
written down in a notebook, learned, and memorized by heart
so they can be thrown in my face. Oh, I feel like weeping
my life away! Here is my dagger,
and here is my bare chest; inside it is a heart   110
more full of riches than Pluto's mine, more precious than gold.
If you're truly a Roman, take this dagger.
You claim that I refused you gold, but I'll give you my heart.
Strike me like you struck Caesar, for I know
that when you hated him most, you loved him more   115
than you ever loved Cassius.

BRUTUS

Put away your dagger.
Be angry all you like, for your anger will always run its course.
Whatever you do, I'll always pass off your insults as quirks of your
   temperament.
Oh, Cassius, you're too much of a lamb to keep this up,   120
for you hold on to your anger like a flint holds on to fire:
when it's forcefully struck, it produces a fleeting spark,
but right away turns cold again.

CASSIUS

Has Cassius lived
to see himself become nothing more than a source of
   merriment and laughter to Brutus,   125
whenever Cassius is troubled by sorrow and bad temper?

BRUTUS

When I said that about you, I was in bad temper, too.

CASSIUS

So you admit it, then? Give me your hand.

   They clasp hands.

---

126   *blood ill-tempered*   a disposition in which the four humors of the body (blood,
   phlegm, choler, and black bile) are not properly "tempered," or in equilibrium

BRUTUS

And my heart too. [*They clasp hands.*]

CASSIUS

130   O Brutus!

BRUTUS

                              What's the matter?

CASSIUS

Have not you love enough to bear with me,
When that rash humor which my mother gave me
Makes me forgetful?

BRUTUS

135   Yes, Cassius, and from henceforth,
When you are over-earnest with your Brutus,
He'll think your mother chides, and leave you so.

> *Enter a* POET [*followed by* LUCILIUS, TITINIUS, *and* LUCIUS].

POET

Let me go in to see the generals.
There is some grudge between 'em; 'tis not meet
140   They be alone.

LUCILIUS

                  You shall not come to them.

POET

Nothing but death shall stay me.

CASSIUS

How now? What's the matter?

POET

For shame, you generals! What do you mean?
145   Love and be friends as two such men should be;
For I have seen more years, I'm sure, than ye.

CASSIUS

Ha, ha! How vilely doth this cynic* rhyme!

---

147   *cynic*   a Cynic philosopher; also a rude, boorish fellow (from the Greek word for dog)

BRUTUS

And my heart, too. (*They clasp hands.*)

CASSIUS

Oh, Brutus! 130

BRUTUS

What's the matter?

CASSIUS

Don't you love me enough to be patient with me
whenever that quick temper I inherited from my mother
gets the best of me?

BRUTUS

Yes, Cassius—and from now on, 135
whenever you are overbearing with your Brutus,
he'll assume that it's your mother talking and let it go at that.

A POET enters, followed by LUCILIUS, TITINIUS, and LUCIUS.

POET

Let me go in to see the generals.
They're having some kind of quarrel; it's not right
for them to be alone. 140

LUCILIUS

You can't go in to see them.

POET

Nothing but death can stop me.

CASSIUS

What's this, what's the matter?

POET

For shame, you generals! What are you thinking?
Love each other and be friends, as two men like yourselves 145
should be,
for I'm sure that I've seen more years than ye.

CASSIUS

Ha, ha! How badly this vulgar fellow rhymes!

BRUTUS

Get you hence, sirrah; saucy fellow, hence!

CASSIUS

Bear with him, Brutus, 'tis his fashion.

BRUTUS

150 I'll know his humor when he knows his time.
What should the wars do with these jigging fools?
Companion, hence!

CASSIUS

Away, away, be gone!

Exit POET.

BRUTUS

Lucilius and Titinius, bid the commanders
155 Prepare to lodge their companies tonight.

CASSIUS

And come yourselves, and bring Messala with you
Immediately to us.

[*Exeunt* LUCILIUS *and* TITINIUS.]

BRUTUS

Lucius, a bowl of wine.

[*Exit* LUCIUS.]

CASSIUS

I did not think you could have been so angry.

BRUTUS

160 O Cassius, I am sick of many griefs.

CASSIUS

Of your philosophy* you make no use,
If you give place to accidental evils.

BRUTUS

No man bears sorrow better. Portia is dead.

CASSIUS

Ha! Portia?

---

161 *philosophy* i.e., Stoicism. As a Stoic, Brutus should be superior to changes in
fortune, since the Stoics believed that no evil should affect a man's inner
tranquility and peace of mind.

BRUTUS

Get out of here, you rascal! Rude fellow, go away!

CASSIUS

Be patient with him, Brutus. It's only his way.

BRUTUS

I'll put up with his ways when he can choose a better time.   150
What use are these rhyming fools in a war?—
Get away, you oaf!

CASSIUS

Get away, get away, be off!

> *The* POET *exits.*

BRUTUS

Lucilius and Titinius, tell the officers
to get their troops ready to camp for the night.   155

CASSIUS

And then come back immediately, and bring
Messala with you.

> LUCIUS *and* TITINIUS *exit.*

BRUTUS

Lucius, bring a bowl of wine.

> LUCIUS *exits.*

CASSIUS

I didn't think that you could be so angry.

BRUTUS

Oh, Cassius, I'm sick from many sorrows.   160

CASSIUS

You're not making use of your philosophy
if you let chance misfortunes get the best of you.

BRUTUS

No man deals with sorrows better than I. Portia is dead.

CASSIUS

What? Portia?

BRUTUS

165   She is dead.

CASSIUS

How scaped I killing when I crossed you so?
O insupportable and touching loss!
Upon what sickness?

BRUTUS

Impatient of my absence,
170   And grief that young Octavius with Mark Antony
Have made themselves so strong—for with her death
That tidings came. With this she fell distract,
And, her attendants absent, swallowed fire.

CASSIUS

And died so?

BRUTUS

175   Even so.

CASSIUS

O ye immortal gods!

Enter BOY [LUCIUS] *with wine and tapers.*

BRUTUS

Speak no more of her.—Give me a bowl of wine.—
In this I bury all unkindness, Cassius.

Drinks.

CASSIUS

My heart is thirsty for that noble pledge.—
180   Fill, Lucius, till the wine o'erswell the cup.
I cannot drink too much of Brutus's love.

[*Exit* LUCIUS.]

Enter TITINIUS *and* MESSALA.

BRUTUS

Come in, Titinius. Welcome, good Messala.
Now sit we close about this taper here,
And call in question our necessities. [*They sit.*]

BRUTUS

She is dead. 165

CASSIUS

How did I escape being killed when I angered you so?
Oh, what an unbearable and painful loss!
What sickness did she die of?

BRUTUS

She couldn't endure my absence
and worried because young Octavius and Mark Antony 170
have made themselves so strong—for news of their increasing
    strength reached me
at the same time as news of her death. She became distraught
    from all this,
and when her servants were away, she swallowed hot coals.

CASSIUS

And she died from that?

BRUTUS

Indeed, she did. 175

CASSIUS

Oh, you immortal gods!

    LUCIUS enters with wine and candles.

BRUTUS

Don't talk about her anymore.—Give me a bowl of wine.—
In this wine, I'll drown all my anger, Cassius.

    He drinks.

CASSIUS

My heart is thirsty to drink to that noble toast.—
Fill the cup, Lucius, until the wine pours over the brim; 180
I cannot drink enough of Brutus's love.

    He drinks. LUCIUS exits. TITINIUS and MESSALA enter.

BRUTUS

Come in, Titinius. Welcome, good Messala.
Let's sit near this candle here
and discuss what needs to be done.

    They sit.

CASSIUS

185   Portia, art thou gone?

BRUTUS

No more, I pray you.—
Messala, I have here received letters
That young Octavius and Mark Antony
Come down upon us with a mighty power,
190   Bending their expedition toward Philippi.*

MESSALA

Myself have letters of the selfsame tenure.

BRUTUS

With what addition?

MESSALA

That by **proscription** and bills of outlawry,
Octavius, Antony, and Lepidus
195   Have put to death an hundred senators.

BRUTUS

Therein our letters do not well agree.
Mine speak of seventy senators that died
By their proscriptions, Cicero being one.

CASSIUS

Cicero one?

MESSALA

200   Cicero is dead,
And by that order of proscription.
Had you your letters from your wife, my lord?*

BRUTUS

No, Messala.

MESSALA

Nor nothing in your letters writ of her?

BRUTUS

205   Nothing, Messala.

---

190   *Philippi*   a city in Macedonia (now northeastern Greece, near the Aegean
seacoast). Philippi was hundreds of miles from Sardis, although Shakespeare
seems to suggest that they are not very far apart.

CASSIUS

Portia, are you really gone? 185

BRUTUS

Say no more, I beg you.—
Messala, I have received these letters
saying that young Octavius and Mark Antony
are approaching us with a mighty army,
marching rapidly toward Philippi. 190

MESSALA

I've received letters saying much the same thing.

BRUTUS

What else do your letters say?

MESSALA

That Octavius, Antony, and Lepidus,
by means of death decrees and lists of those condemned,
have put a hundred senators to death. 195

BRUTUS

Our letters differ about that.
Mine say that seventy senators have died
by those decrees—and Cicero is one.

CASSIUS

Cicero is one?

MESSALA

Cicero is dead 200
because of such a decree.
Did you receive letters from your wife, my lord?

BRUTUS

No, Messala.

MESSALA

Nor did any letters you received say anything about her?

BRUTUS

Nothing, Messala. 205

202-17   This second revelation of Portia's death conflicts with the earlier account in
this scene. It seems to be the original version that was later revised. Perhaps it
was meant to be deleted but editors overlooked it.

MESSALA

That methinks is strange.

BRUTUS

Why ask you? Hear you aught of her in yours?

MESSALA

No, my lord.

BRUTUS

Now as you are a Roman, tell me true.

MESSALA

210 Then like a Roman bear the truth I tell;
For certain she is dead, and by strange manner.

BRUTUS

Why, farewell, Portia. We must die, Messala.
With meditating that she must die once,
I have the patience to endure it now.

MESSALA

215 Even so great men great losses should endure.

CASSIUS

I have as much of this in art as you,
But yet my nature could not bear it so.

BRUTUS

Well, to our work alive. What do you think
Of marching to Philippi presently?

CASSIUS

220 I do not think it good.

BRUTUS

Your reason?

CASSIUS

This it is:
'Tis better that the enemy seek us;
So shall he waste his means, weary his soldiers,
225 Doing himself offense, whilst we, lying still,
Are full of rest, defense, and nimbleness.

BRUTUS

Good reasons must of force give place to better.
The people 'twixt Philippi and this ground

MESSALA
I find that strange.

BRUTUS
Why do you ask? Did you hear anything about her in your letters?

MESSALA
No, my lord.

BRUTUS
If you are a Roman, tell me the truth, now.

MESSALA
Then take the truth I'm about to tell you like a Roman—   210
for she has certainly died and in a strange way.

BRUTUS
Well, farewell, Portia. We all must die, Messala.
Because I have thought about her dying
gives me the patience to endure her death.

MESSALA
This is exactly how great men should endure great losses.   215

CASSIUS
I've studied as much Stoic philosophy as you,
and yet my character couldn't endure such a loss this way.

BRUTUS
Well, let those of us who live get to work. What do you think
of our marching immediately to Philippi?

CASSIUS
I don't think it's a good idea.   220

BRUTUS
What's your reason for thinking so?

CASSIUS
It's this:
It's better for the enemy to have to look for us;
that way, he'll waste his supplies, exhaust his soldiers,
and do himself harm—while we, by keeping still,   225
will remain rested, well-defended, and alert.

BRUTUS
Good reasons must necessarily make way for better reasons.
The people between Philippi and here

230 Do stand but in a forced affection;
For they have grudged us contribution.
The enemy, marching along by them,
By them shall make a fuller number up,
Come on refreshed, new added, and encouraged;
235 From which advantage shall we cut him off
If at Philippi we do face him there,
These people at our back.

CASSIUS

Hear me, good brother.—

BRUTUS

Under your pardon. You must note beside
That we have tried the utmost of our friends,
240 Our legions are brimful, our cause is ripe.
The enemy increaseth every day;
We, at the height, are ready to decline.
There is a tide in the affairs of men,
Which, taken at the flood, leads on to fortune;
245 Omitted, all the voyage of their life
Is bound in shallows and in miseries.
On such a full sea are we now afloat,
And we must take the current when it serves,
Or lose our ventures.

CASSIUS

250 Then, with your will, go on.
We'll along ourselves and meet them at Philippi.

BRUTUS

The deep of the night is crept upon our talk,
And nature must obey necessity,
Which we will niggard with a little rest.
255 There is no more to say?

CASSIUS

No more. Good night.

[*They stand.*]

Early tomorrow will we rise, and hence.

are loyal to us only because they're forced to be,
for they have given us money grudgingly.   230
If our enemies march among them,
they'll be able to increase their numbers
and arrive refreshed, reinforced, and full of courage;
we can stop them from getting this advantage
if we face them at Philippi,   235
with these people behind us.

CASSIUS
Listen to me, good brother—

BRUTUS
Excuse me, let me finish. You must also consider
that we have demanded all we can expect from our friends.
Our troops are plentiful, and our best time is now.   240
The enemy grows stronger everyday.
We're at our strongest and will soon grow weaker.
The business of men follows a changing tide:
setting sail at high tide leads to good fortune;
if the high tide is missed, life's voyage   245
leads only to shallow water and misery.
We are now afloat on a great sea,
and we must make use of the tide when it's best for us
or else lose our cargo.

CASSIUS
Then we'll go on, as you wish.   250
We'll march forth and meet the enemy at Philippi.

BRUTUS
We've talked late into the night,
and because we are human, we need some sleep;
we'll be stingy with ourselves and sleep only a little.
Is there anything else to say?   255

CASSIUS
Nothing else. Good night.

> *They rise from their chairs.*

Early tomorrow morning, we'll wake up and go.

BRUTUS
Lucius! [*Enter* LUCIUS.]
My gown. [*Exit* LUCIUS.]
Farewell, good Messala.—
260 Good night, Titinius.—Noble, noble Cassius,
Good night, and good repose.

CASSIUS
O my dear brother,
This was an ill beginning of the night.
Never come such division 'tween our souls!
265 Let it not, Brutus.

Enter LUCIUS *with the gown.*

BRUTUS
Everything is well.

CASSIUS
Good night, my lord.

BRUTUS
Good night, good brother.

TITINIUS, MESSALA
Good night, Lord Brutus.

BRUTUS
270 Farewell every one.

Exeunt [CASSIUS, TITINIUS, *and* MESSALA].

Give me the gown. Where is thy instrument?*

LUCIUS
Here in the tent.

BRUTUS
What, thou speak'st drowsily?
Poor knave, I blame thee not; thou art o'erwatched.
275 Call Claudio and some other of my men;
I'll have them sleep on cushions in my tent.

---

271 *instrument* probably a lute or some related stringed instrument

BRUTUS

Lucius.

    LUCIUS enters.

Bring me my gown.

    LUCIUS exits.

Farewell, good Messala.—
Good night, Titinius.—Noble, noble Cassius,   260
good night and sleep well.

CASSIUS

Oh, my dear brother,
this was a bad way to start the night.
Let's never again allow such a quarrel to come between us!
Let's not allow it, Brutus.   265

    LUCIUS enters with the gown.

BRUTUS

Everything is fine.

CASSIUS

Good night, my lord.

BRUTUS

Good night, good brother.

TITINIUS, MESSALA

Good night, Lord Brutus.

BRUTUS

Farewell, everyone.   270

    All but BRUTUS and LUCIUS exit.

Give me my gown. Where is your lute?

LUCIUS

Here in the tent.

BRUTUS

Why do you sound so sleepy?
Poor lad, I don't blame you; you're exhausted from lack of
    sleep.
Call Claudio and some of my other men;   275
I'll have them sleep on cushions in my tent.

LUCIUS
Varrus and Claudio!

Enter VARRUS *and* CLAUDIO.

VARRUS
Calls my lord?

BRUTUS
I pray you, sirs, lie in my tent and sleep;
280   It may be I shall raise you by and by
On business to my brother Cassius.

VARRUS
So please you, we will stand and watch your pleasure.

BRUTUS
I will not have it so. Lie down, good sirs.
It may be I shall otherwise bethink me.

[*They lie down.*]

285   Look, Lucius, here's the book I sought for so;
I put it in the pocket of my gown.

LUCIUS
I was sure your lordship did not give it me.

BRUTUS
Bear with me, good boy, I am much forgetful.
Canst thou hold up thy heavy eyes awhile,
290   And touch thy instrument a strain or two?

LUCIUS
Ay, my lord, an 't please you.

BRUTUS
                   It does, my boy.
I trouble thee too much, but thou art willing.

LUCIUS
It is my duty, sir.

BRUTUS
295   I should not urge thy duty past thy might;
I know young bloods look for a time of rest.

LUCIUS
I have slept, my lord, already.

LUCIUS

Varrus and Claudio!

VARRUS and CLAUDIO enter.

VARRUS

Did my lord call for us?

BRUTUS

Sirs, I ask you to lie in my tent and sleep here.
It may be that I'll wake you up by and by   280
to send you on business to my brother Cassius.

VARRUS

If you wish, we'll stand here and stay awake for your commands.

BRUTUS

I won't allow that. Lie down, good sirs.
It may be that I'll change my mind.

They lie down.

Look, Lucius—here's the book I was searching for.   285
I put it in the pocket of my gown.

LUCIUS

I was sure that your lordship didn't give it to me.

BRUTUS

Be patient with me, good boy; I am very forgetful.
Can you keep your tired eyes open awhile longer
and play a tune or two on your instrument?   290

LUCIUS

Yes, my lord, if it pleases you.

BRUTUS

It does, my boy.
I'm putting you to too much trouble, but you're willing.

LUCIUS

It is my duty, sir.

BRUTUS

I shouldn't expect you to do your duty beyond your strength.   295
I know that young people need time to rest.

LUCIUS

I have slept already, my lord.

BRUTUS
It was well done, and thou shalt sleep again;
I will not hold thee long. If I do live,
300   I will be good to thee.

        Music and a song.

This is a sleepy tune. O murd'rous slumber!*
Layest thou thy leaden mace upon my boy,
That plays thee music?—Gentle knave, good night.
I will not do thee so much wrong to wake thee.
305   If thou dost nod, thou break'st thy instrument;
I'll take it from thee and, good boy, good night.

        [*He moves the instrument.*]

Let me see, let me see. Is not the leaf turned down
Where I left reading? Here it is, I think.
How ill this taper burns.

        Enter the GHOST OF CAESAR.

310   Ha! Who comes here?—
I think it is the weakness of mine eyes
That shapes this monstrous apparition.
It comes upon me.—Art thou any thing?
Art thou some god, some angel, or some devil,
315   That mak'st my blood cold and my hair to stare?
Speak to me what thou art.

GHOST
Thy evil spirit, Brutus.

BRUTUS
                    Why com'st thou?

GHOST
To tell thee thou shalt see me at Philippi.

BRUTUS
320   Well; then I shall see thee again?

GHOST
Ay, at Philippi.

---

murd'rous slumber Sleep is, conventionally, an image of death.

BRUTUS
That was a good thing to do, and you will sleep again.
I won't keep you up long. And if I survive this battle,
I'll continue being good to you. 300

> LUCIUS *plays and sings a song, then falls asleep.*

This is a sleepy tune. Oh, death-like sleep,
do you touch my boy with your lead staff
while he's playing music for you?
(*to* LUCIUS) Gentle lad, good night.
I won't do you the wrong of waking you up.
But if you bend over, you'll break your instrument. 305
I'll take it away from you. And good night, good boy.

> *He takes the lute.*

Let me see, let me see; isn't the page turned down
where I stopped reading? Here it is, I think.
How badly this candle burns.

> *The* GHOST OF CAESAR *enters.*

Oh!—who comes here? 310
I think my weak eyes
must make me see this monstrous apparition.
It's coming toward me.
(*to the* GHOST) Do you really exist?
Are you some god, some angel, or some devil,
that you make my blood run cold and my hair stand on end? 315
Tell me what you are.

GHOST
Your evil spirit, Brutus.

BRUTUS
Why have you come?

GHOST
To tell you that you will see me at Philippi.

BRUTUS
Well, then. I'll see you again? 320

GHOST
Yes, at Philippi.

BRUTUS

Why, I will see thee at Philippi then.

[*Exit* GHOST.]

Now I have taken heart, thou vanishest.
Ill spirit, I would hold more talk with thee.
325 Boy! Lucius! Varrus! Claudio! Sirs, awake!
Claudio!

LUCIUS

The strings, my lord, are false.

BRUTUS

He thinks he still is at his instrument.
Lucius, awake!

LUCIUS

330 My lord?

BRUTUS

Didst thou dream, Lucius, that thou so criedst out?

LUCIUS

My lord, I do not know that I did cry.

BRUTUS

Yes, that thou didst. Didst thou see anything?

LUCIUS

Nothing, my lord.

BRUTUS

335 Sleep again, Lucius.—Sirrah Claudio!
[*to Varrus*] Fellow thou, awake!

[*They rise up.*]

VARRUS

My lord.

CLAUDIO

My lord.

BRUTUS

Why did you so cry out, sirs, in your sleep?

BOTH

340 Did we, my lord?

BRUTUS

Why, I will see you at Philippi then.

The GHOST *exits.*

Now that I have regained my courage, you've vanished.
Evil spirit, I wish I could talk more with you.—
Boy! Lucius! Varrus! Claudio! Sirs, awake!   325
Claudio!

LUCIUS

The strings are out of tune, my lord.

BRUTUS

He thinks he's still playing his lute.
Lucius, wake up!

LUCIUS

My lord?   330

BRUTUS

Were you dreaming when you cried out, Lucius?

LUCIUS

My lord, I didn't know I cried out.

BRUTUS

Yes, you did. Did you see anything?

LUCIUS

Nothing, my lord.

BRUTUS

Go back to sleep, Lucius.—Claudio, my friend!   335
Varrus, old fellow! Wake up!

They wake up.

VARRUS

My lord?

CLAUDIO

My lord?

BRUTUS

Why did you cry out in your sleep, sirs?

VARRUS, CLAUDIO

Did we, my lord?   340

BRUTUS

Ay. Saw you anything?

VARRUS

No, my lord, I saw nothing.

CLAUDIO

Nor I, my lord.

BRUTUS

Go and commend me to my brother Cassius.
345 Bid him set on his powers betimes before,
And we will follow.

BOTH

It shall be done, my lord.

Exeunt.

BRUTUS
Yes. Did you see anything?

VARRUS
No, my lord, I didn't see anything.

CLAUDIO
Nor I, my lord.

BRUTUS
Go and take my greetings to my brother Cassius.
Tell him to march out with his army early this morning   345
    before me,
and we'll follow after him.

VARRUS, CLAUDIO
We shall do it, my lord.

They all exit.

Act IV Review

Discussion Questions

1. What is your opinion of Lepidus in the first scene of this act?

2. Why do you think Cassius and Brutus quarrel?

3. What effect would you say is gained by the revelation of Portia's death?

4. If Brutus were able to go back in time and decide all over again whether to participate in the conspiracy, what do you think he would do and why?

5. How has Antony changed since he delivered the funeral oration? Think about how his actions, words, and goals are different. Look in Act IV for specific examples that back up your views.

6. How does the Second Triumvirate compare to the conspirators?

Literary Elements

1. A **tragedy** is a serious work of literature that narrates the events leading to the downfall of a **tragic hero**, who displays noble qualities but also has a **tragic flaw** or fatal character weakness. How does Brutus fit this definition? Name his tragic flaw.

2. Study the **dialogue** in Scene iii between Brutus and Cassius regarding Portia's death (lines 163–178). What does each man's reaction say about his character?

3. **Imagery** refers to word pictures that appeal to the five senses and add emotion and power to the writing. In Scene ii, line 21, Brutus refers to Cassius as "a hot friend cooling." Does this **imagery** strike you as an effective way to describe the relationship between the two men? Explain why or why not.

4. A **metaphor** is a figure of speech that makes a comparison between things that are not truly alike. An **extended metaphor** is a complex comparison that goes on for several lines. Explain the extended metaphor comparing men to horses in Scene ii, lines 25–29, or the one involving the sea in Scene iii, lines 243–249.

Writing Prompts

1. In Scene i, Antony compares Lepidus to two animals. Suggest an animal that Caesar, Brutus, and Antony each remind you of. Give one or two reasons for your choices.

2. After their bitter argument, Cassius says to Brutus, "O my dear brother ... Never come such division 'tween our souls! / Let it not, Brutus." Think about fights between people you know. Do you believe that arguments can ever strengthen a friendship, or do you think that true friends never disagree? From events in your own life, write about a fight or argument that made a friendship either stronger or weaker.

3. Choose a scene and write a brief summary of its events in one sentence. You may choose to write it in standard English, contemporary slang or street talk, or the language of Shakespeare, Elizabethan English. Or write three summaries; use a separate style in each.

4. Choose a quotation from one of the scenes in Act IV that you feel best characterizes that scene. In a paragraph, discuss why you think this quotation is significant and effective at conveying the events or emotions of the scene.

Julius Caesar

Act V

Battle of Philippi in Joseph L. Mankiewicz's *Julius Caesar*, 1953

"O Julius Caesar, thou art mighty yet!
Thy spirit walks abroad and turns our swords
In our own proper entrails."

Before You Read

1. Why do you think Shakespeare has continued his play beyond Caesar's assassination? Consider why the play is called *Julius Caesar*.

2. Do you believe that deeds such as murder will inevitably be punished one way or another? Explain your answer.

3. What do you think would be a just and fair conclusion to this play for everyone concerned?

Literary Elements

1. As you may recall, **dramatic conflict** is the struggle between opposing forces within a play. In Act III, Mark Antony's display of Caesar's corpse leads to more dramatic conflict between the angry citizens and the conspirators. Enraged, the citizens march on the homes of Brutus and his allies.

2. **Personification** means attributing human characteristics to nonhuman things. In Act I, Casca personifies the ocean by saying, " …I have seen / Th' ambitious ocean swell and rage and foam …"

3. **Mood**, or atmosphere, refers to the feelings the audience has toward the events of the play. The mood in Act I becomes ominous during the stormy night when Cassius and Casca plot to destroy Caesar.

4. A word or phrase that can mean more than one thing or be taken two ways is a **double entendre**. In Shakespeare's time, the medical condition of epilepsy was called the "falling sickness." When Brutus speculates in Act I that Caesar has this, Cassius tells him, "No, Caesar hath it not, but you, and I, and honest Casca, we have the falling sickness." Cassius means that he and the others are too willing to fall down before Caesar, therefore giving him too much power.

Words to Know

The following vocabulary words appear in Act V in the original text of Shakespeare's play. However, they are words that are still commonly used. Read the definitions here and pay attention to the words as you read the play (they will be in boldfaced type).

consorted	associated; kept company
disconsolate	sad; dejected
engendered [engend'red]	produced; brought about
exigent	critical moment; a demanding time
gallant	splendid; spirited
misconstrued	made a mistake; misunderstood
peevish	irritable; crabby
presage	predict; foretell
providence	will; guiding power
reveler	partygoer; merrymaker
suffices [sufficeth]	satisfies; is adequate

Act Summary

To Romans, a parley—or meeting—between military opponents offered an important chance to discuss tactics and take stock of their opponents. As Scene i opens, Antony and Octavius parley with Brutus and Cassius to discuss the upcoming battle. Octavius refuses to follow Antony's command, and all four of the leaders argue and criticize one another. After the other generals have departed, Brutus and Cassius exchange emotional farewells, which seems to foreshadow their defeat at Philippi.

As the battle proceeds, Cassius becomes convinced of his doom and orders Pindarus to kill him. Distraught at finding Cassius dead, loyal Titinius kills himself. Brutus comes upon the gory scene and claims to feel the spirit of Caesar, avenging his own death and the spirit of Rome.

Finally, Brutus's troops are overpowered by Antony's. Disheartened, Brutus urges each of his comrades to kill him off, but all refuse. Finally Strato agrees to hold a sword while Brutus runs on it. Antony and Octavius arrive, and Antony declares Brutus "the noblest Roman of them all. . . . This was a man!"

Mark Antony (Marlon Brando) stands over the dead Brutus (James Mason), Mankiewicz film, 1953

ACT V, SCENE I

[*Near Philippi*]. *Enter* OCTAVIUS, ANTONY, *and their* ARMY.

OCTAVIUS

Now, Antony, our hopes are answered.
You said the enemy would not come down,
But keep the hills and upper regions.
It proves not so. Their battles are at hand;
They mean to warn us at Philippi here,
Answering before we do demand of them.

ANTONY

Tut, I am in their bosoms, and I know
Wherefore they do it. They could be content
To visit other places, and come down
With fearful bravery, thinking by this face
To fasten in our thoughts that they have courage;
But 'tis not so.

Enter a MESSENGER.

MESSENGER

            Prepare you, generals;
The enemy comes on in **gallant** show.
Their bloody sign of battle is hung out,
And something to be done immediately.

ANTONY

Octavius, lead your battle softly on
Upon the left hand of the even field.

OCTAVIUS

Upon the right hand I; keep thou the left.

ANTONY

Why do you cross me in this **exigent**?

OCTAVIUS

I do not cross you; but I will do so.

March.

Drum. Enter BRUTUS, CASSIUS, *and their* ARMY;
[LUCILIUS, TITINIUS, MESSALA, *and others*].

ACT 5, SCENE 1

The plains of Philippi. OCTAVIUS, ANTONY, *and their* ARMY *enter.*

OCTAVIUS
Our hopes have now been fulfilled, Antony.
You said that the enemy would not come down,
but would stay in the hills and the higher areas.
This turns out not to be so. Their armies are near.
They intend to challenge us right here at Philippi,   5
answering our call to battle before we even make it.

ANTONY
Never mind, I know their every thought, so I know
why they are doing this. They really wish
they were someplace else, but they come down
acting bravely and trying to inspire fear, supposing that
    by this outward display,   10
they will convince us that they have courage.
But they don't.

    A MESSENGER *enters.*

MESSENGER
Get ready, generals.
The enemy comes toward us with a splendid display.
They've hung out their red flag of battle   15
and are about to do something right away.

ANTONY
Octavius, lead your army slowly
along the left side of the level field.

OCTAVIUS
I'll march on the right side; you keep to the left.

ANTONY
Why do you contradict me in this crisis?   20

OCTAVIUS
I don't contradict you, but I will do as I please.

    Their ARMY *marches. Drums.* BRUTUS, CASSIUS, *and their*
    ARMY *enter, along with* LUCILIUS, TITINIUS, *and* MESSALA.

BRUTUS

They stand and would have parley.

CASSIUS

Stand fast, Titinius. We must out and talk.

OCTAVIUS

Mark Antony, shall we give sign of battle?

ANTONY

25 No, Caesar, we will answer on their charge.
Make forth. The generals would have some words.

OCTAVIUS [*to his* OFFICERS]

Stir not until the signal.

[*The* GENERALs *step forward.*]

BRUTUS

Words before blows. Is it so, countrymen?

OCTAVIUS

Not that we love words better, as you do.

BRUTUS

30 Good words are better than bad strokes, Octavius.

ANTONY

In your bad strokes, Brutus, you give good words;
Witness the hole you made in Caesar's heart,
Crying, "Long live! Hail, Caesar!"

CASSIUS

                          Antony,

35 The posture of your blows are yet unknown;
But for your words, they rob the Hybla* bees,
And leave them honeyless.

ANTONY

Not stingless too.

BRUTUS

O yes, and soundless too,
40 For you have stol'n their buzzing, Antony,
And very wisely threat before you sting.

---

36 *Hybla* a mountain in Sicily and a town proverbially famous for its honey

BRUTUS
They've stopped and want to hold a conference.

CASSIUS
Stay right here, Titinius. Brutus and I must go and talk with them.

OCTAVIUS
Mark Antony, shall we give the signal to attack?

ANTONY
No, Caesar, we'll meet them when they attack.   25
Go forward. The generals want to talk with us.

OCTAVIUS (*to his* OFFICERS)
Don't move until you get the signal.

      The GENERALS *move toward each other.*

BRUTUS
We'll exchange words before blows. Is that right, countrymen?

OCTAVIUS
Not that we love words better than blows, like you do.

BRUTUS
Good words are better than bad blows, Octavius.   30

ANTONY
You speak good words while you give bad blows, Brutus.
Remember the hole you made in Caesar's heart,
even while you cried, "Long live Caesar! Hail, Caesar!"

CASSIUS
Antony,
we don't yet know what kinds of blows you'll give,   35
but as for your sweet words, they rob the Hybla bees,
leaving them without honey.

ANTONY
But not without their sting.

BRUTUS
Oh, yes—and without sound as well
for you have stolen their buzzing, Antony,   40
and very wisely buzz threats at us before you sting.

ANTONY
Villains, you did not so when your vile daggers
Hacked one another in the sides of Caesar.
You showed your teeth like apes, and fawned like hounds,
And bowed like bondmen, kissing Caesar's feet;
Whilst damned Casca, like a cur, behind
Struck Caesar on the neck. O you flatterers!

CASSIUS
Flatterers?—Now, Brutus, thank yourself;
This tongue had not offended so today
If Cassius might have ruled.

OCTAVIUS
Come, come, the cause. If arguing make us sweat,
The proof of it will turn to redder drops.
Look, I draw a sword against conspirators;

[*He draws.*]

When think you that the sword goes up again?
Never till Caesar's three and thirty wounds
Be well avenged, or till another Caesar
Have added slaughter to the sword of traitors.

BRUTUS
Caesar, thou canst not die by traitors' hands
Unless thou bring'st them with thee.

OCTAVIUS
                                    So I hope.
I was not born to die on Brutus's sword.

BRUTUS
O if thou wert the noblest of thy strain,
Young man, thou couldst not die more honorable.

CASSIUS
A **peevish** schoolboy, worthless of such honor,
Joined with a masker and a **reveler**.

ANTONY
Old Cassius still.

ANTONY

Villains, you didn't do so when your filthy daggers
hacked one another in Caesar's sides.
You grinned like apes, cringed like hounds,
and bowed like servants, kissing Caesar's feet,   45
while damned Casca, like a vicious dog, struck Caesar
in the neck from behind. Oh, you flatterers!

CASSIUS

Flatterers! Now, Brutus, you've got only yourself to thank for this.
Antony's tongue wouldn't have spoken so offensively today
if Cassius had had his way.   50

OCTAVIUS

Come on, come on, let's get down to business. If arguing makes us
    sweat,
putting our argument to the test will bring redder drops.
Look, I draw my sword against the conspirators.

He draws his sword.

When do you think I'll sheathe this sword again?
Never—or not until Caesar's thirty-three wounds   55
are completely avenged, or until another Caesar
has been slain by traitors' swords.

BRUTUS

Caesar, you cannot die by a traitors' hands,
unless you die by your own hands.

OCTAVIUS

I hope I do.   60
I wasn't born to die by Brutus's sword.

BRUTUS

Oh, if you were the noblest member of your family,
young man, you couldn't die a more honorable death.

CASSIUS (*to* BRUTUS)

He's a childish schoolboy who doesn't deserve such an honor.
And Antony is a party-goer who loves masquerades!   65

ANTONY

You're still the same old Cassius.

OCTAVIUS

Come, Antony. Away!
Defiance, traitors, hurl we in your teeth.
If you dare fight today, come to the field;
70 If not, when you have stomachs.

Exit OCTAVIUS, ANTONY, *and* ARMY.

CASSIUS

Why now, blow wind, swell billow, and swim bark!
The storm is up, and all is on the hazard.

BRUTUS

Ho, Lucilius, hark, a word with you.

LUCILIUS *and* MESSALA *stand forth.*

LUCILIUS

My lord?

[BRUTUS *and* LUCILIUS *speak apart.*]

CASSIUS

75 Messala.

MESSALA *stands forth.*

MESSALA

What says my general?

CASSIUS

Messala,
This is my birthday, as this very day
Was Cassius born. Give me thy hand, Messala.
80 Be thou my witness that against my will,
As Pompey was, am I compelled to set
Upon one battle all our liberties.
You know that I held Epicurus* strong,
And his opinion. Now I change my mind,
85 And partly credit things that do **presage**.
Coming from Sardis, on our former ensign

---

83 *Epicurus* The Epicurean philosophy was strongly materialistic and assumed that
the gods do not trouble themselves about human affairs. Omens and portents,
therefore, are of no significance and should be ignored.

OCTAVIUS
Come on, Antony, let's go!
Traitors, we throw our defiance in your teeth.
If you dare to fight today, come to the field;
if not, come whenever you've worked up the nerve.   70

> OCTAVIUS, ANTONY, *and their* ARMY *exit.*

CASSIUS
Well, now—let the winds blow, the waves rise, and the ship
   set sail!
The storm has come, and everything is at stake.

BRUTUS
Lucilius, listen—I want a word with you.

> LUCILIUS *and* MESSALA *step forward.*

LUCILIUS
My lord?

> BRUTUS *and* LUCILIUS *go to one side and talk.*

CASSIUS
Messala.   75

MESSALA
What do you have to say, general?

CASSIUS
Messala,
this is my birthday—for on this very day,
Cassius was born. Give me your hand, Messala.
Be my witness that I'm being forced   80
against my will to gamble everything we've achieved
on just one battle—just as Pompey once was forced to do.
You know that I've always believed strongly
in the opinions of Epicurus. But now I change my mind
and partly believe in some prophetic events.   85
While we were coming here from Sardis, two mighty eagles
   lighted

Two mighty eagles fell, and there they perched,
Gorging and feeding from our soldiers' hands,
Who to Philippi here **consorted** us.
90 This morning are they fled away and gone,
And in their steads do ravens, crows, and kites
Fly o'er our heads and downward look on us
As we were sickly prey. Their shadows seem
A canopy most fatal, under which
95 Our army lies, ready to give up the ghost.

MESSALA
Believe not so.

CASSIUS
                    I but believe it partly,
For I am fresh of spirit and resolved
To meet all perils very constantly.

BRUTUS
100 Even so, Lucilius.

CASSIUS
                    Now, most noble Brutus,
The gods today stand friendly, that we may,
Lovers in peace, lead on our days to age.
But since the affairs of men rests still incertain,
105 Let's reason with the worst that may befall.
If we do lose this battle, then is this
The very last time we shall speak together.
What are you then determined to do?

BRUTUS
Even by the rule of that philosophy
110 By which I did blame Cato* for the death
Which he did give himself—I know not how,
But I do find it cowardly and vile,
For fear of what might fall, so to prevent
The time of life—arming myself with patience

---

110 *Cato* Marcus Cato, Portia's father, who, after the defeat of Pompey at Pharsalia,
fought on and finally killed himself at Utica in 46 B.C. rather than submit to
Caesar.

on our main banner; and there they perched,
eating and stuffing themselves from our soldiers' hands
and accompanied us here to Philippi.
This morning, they have fled and gone away, 90
and instead of them, ravens, crows, and buzzards
fly over our heads and look down at us
as if we were dying prey. Their shadows seem like
a deadly canopy, under which
our army lies, ready to perish. 95

MESSALA
Don't believe that.

CASSIUS
I only partly believe it,
for my spirits are rested, and I'm determined
to meet all dangers unwaveringly.

BRUTUS
That's fine, Lucilius. 100

BRUTUS *goes back to* CASSIUS.

CASSIUS
Now, most noble Brutus,
may the gods be friendly to us today so that we may
grow old and remain friends in peace.
But since the affairs of men are always uncertain,
let's plan what to do if the worst happens. 105
If we lose this battle, then this
is the very last time we will speak together.
What are you determined to do then?

BRUTUS
I'll follow the rules of my philosophy,
which caused me to criticize Cato for putting himself 110
to death. I don't know why,
but I find it villainous and cowardly
to cut one's own life short for fear
of what might happen. So I'll arm myself with patience

115 To stay the **providence** of some high powers
That govern us below.

CASSIUS
Then, if we lose this battle,
You are contented to be led in triumph
Thorough the streets of Rome?

BRUTUS
120 No, Cassius, no. Think not, thou noble Roman,
That ever Brutus will go bound to Rome;
He bears too great a mind. But this same day
Must end that work the ides of March begun.
And whether we shall meet again I know not;
125 Therefore our everlasting farewell take:
For ever and for ever farewell, Cassius.
If we do meet again, why, we shall smile;
If not, why then this parting was well made.

CASSIUS
For ever and for ever farewell, Brutus.
130 If we do meet again, we'll smile indeed;
If not, 'tis true this parting was well made.

BRUTUS
Why then, lead on. O that a man might know
The end of this day's business ere it come!
But it **sufficeth** that the day will end,
135 And then the end is known. Come, ho! Away!

Exeunt.

and await the fate planned for me by the higher powers   115
that rule us here below.

CASSIUS

So if we lose this battle,
you'll be content to be led in a victory parade
through the streets of Rome?

BRUTUS

No, Cassius, no. You noble Roman, don't think   120
that Brutus will ever return to Rome in chains.
His mind is too proud. But the work
that was begun on the ides of March must be finished today.
And I don't know whether we will meet again.
So let's take our final farewell now.   126
Farewell, for ever and ever, Cassius.
If we meet again—well, we'll smile about this;
if we don't meet, then this parting was the right thing to do.

CASSIUS

Farewell, for ever and ever, Brutus.
If we meet again, we'll certainly smile;   130
if we don't, it's true that this parting was the right thing to do.

BRUTUS

Lead the way, then. Oh, if only a man could know
the end of this day's business before it came!
But it's enough that the day will end,
and that the end will then be known. Come on, let's go!   135

They exit.

ACT V, SCENE II

[*Near Philippi; the field of battle.*] *Alarum. Enter*
BRUTUS *and* MESSALA.

BRUTUS

Ride, ride, Messala, ride, and give these bills
Unto the legions on the other side.

Loud alarum.

Let them set on at once; for I perceive
But cold demeanor in Octavius's wing,
And sudden push gives them the overthrow.
Ride, ride, Messala; let them all come down.

Exeunt.

ACT 5, SCENE 2

Near Philippi, the battlefield. A call to arms is played on drums and trumpets. BRUTUS *and* MESSALA *enter.*

BRUTUS
Ride, ride, Messala, ride—and take these written orders
over to those troops commanded by Cassius.

He gives MESSALA *the orders; drums and trumpets grow louder.*

Let them attack at once, for I can see
that Octavius's troops lack fighting spirit,
and a sudden assault will defeat them.   5
Ride, ride, Messala! Let the whole army come down.

ACT V, SCENE III

[*Another part of the field.*] *Alarums. Enter* CASSIUS *and* TITINIUS.

CASSIUS

O look, Titinius, look, the villains fly!
Myself have to mine own turned enemy.
This ensign here of mine was turning back;
I slew the coward, and did take it from him.

TITINIUS

5   O Cassius, Brutus gave the word too early,
Who, having some advantage on Octavius,
Took it too eagerly. His soldiers fell to spoil,
Whilst we by Antony are all enclosed.

Enter PINDARUS.

PINDARUS

Fly further off, my lord, fly further off;
10   Mark Antony is in your tents, my lord.
Fly, therefore, noble Cassius, fly far off.

CASSIUS

This hill is far enough. Look, look, Titinius.
Are those my tents where I perceive the fire?

TITINIUS

They are, my lord.

CASSIUS

15   Titinius, if thou lovest me,
Mount thou my horse, and hide thy spurs in him
Till he have brought thee up to yonder troops
And here again, that I may rest assured
Whether yond troops are friend or enemy.

TITINIUS

20   I will be here again even with a thought.

Exit.

CASSIUS

Go, Pindarus, get higher on that hill;

ACT 5, SCENE 3

Another part of the battlefield. Drums and trumpets. CASSIUS and TITINIUS enter, CASSIUS carrying a banner.

CASSIUS

Oh look, Titinius, look, the cowards are fleeing!
I've turned into my own men's enemy.
My flag-bearer was turning to go back;
I slew the coward and took the flag away from him.

TITINIUS

Oh, Cassius, Brutus gave the command too early,   5
for when he saw that we had some advantage over Octavius,
he seized it too eagerly. His soldiers fell to looting,
while we've been completely surrounded by Antony's troops.

> *PINDARUS enters.*

PINDARUS

Retreat farther off, my lord, retreat farther off!
Mark Antony has reached your tents, my lord.   10
Therefore retreat, noble Cassius, retreat farther off.

CASSIUS

This hill is far enough. Look, look, Titinius,
are those my tents where I see fire?

TITINIUS

They are, my lord.

CASSIUS

Titinius, if you love me,   15
mount my horse and dig your spurs in him
until he takes you to those troops over there,
then brings you back again so I may know for certain
whether those troops are friend or enemy.

TITINIUS

I'll be back again as quickly as a thought.   20

> *He exits.*

CASSIUS

Go, Pindarus, climb higher on that hill.

My sight was ever thick. Regard Titinius,
And tell me what thou not'st about the field.

    [*Exit* PINDARUS.]

This day I breathed first: time is come round,
25   And where I did begin, there shall I end;
My life is run his compass.—Sirrah, what news?

PINDARUS
(*above*) O my lord!

CASSIUS
What news?

PINDARUS
Titinius is enclosed round about
30   With horsemen that make to him on the spur;
Yet he spurs on. Now they are almost on him.
Now, Titinius! Now some light. O he lights too!
He's ta'en. (*Shout*) And hark, they shout for joy.

CASSIUS
Come down; behold no more.—
35   O coward that I am to live so long
To see my best friend ta'en before my face.

    PINDARUS [*comes down*].

Come hither, sirrah.
In Parthia did I take thee prisoner;
And then I swore thee, saving of thy life,
40   That whatsoever I did bid thee do,
Thou shouldst attempt it. Come now, keep thine oath;
Now be a freeman, and with this good sword
That ran through Caesar's bowels, search this bosom.
Stand not to answer. Here, take thou the hilts;
45   And when my face is covered, as 'tis now,

I've always had bad eyesight. Watch Titinius,
and tell me whatever you can observe about the field.

> PINDARUS *exits.*

This is the day when I first breathed. Time has come around,
and I'll end exactly where I began;   25
my life has run its course.

> PINDARUS *reenters above.*

Fellow, what news?

PINDARUS
Oh, my lord!

CASSIUS
What news?

PINDARUS
Titinius is completely surrounded
by horsemen approaching him at a full gallop,   30
and yet he gallops on. Now they've almost caught up with him.
Now they've reached Titinius! Now some dismount. Oh, he
    dismounts too.
He's been taken. (*shouting*) And listen—they're shouting for joy.

CASSIUS
Come down, don't look anymore.
Oh, what a coward I am to have lived long enough   35
to see my best friend taken prisoner in front of my face!

> PINDARUS *comes down.*

Come here, fellow.
I took you prisoner in Parthia;
and when I saved your life, I made you promise
to try to do   40
whatever I asked you to do. Come now, and keep your promise.
Be a free man now—and with this good sword
that ran through Caesar's belly, pierce this breast.
Don't wait to reply. Here, take hold of the hilt,
and when I've covered my face—as I have now—   45

45　　Guide thou the sword. [PINDARUS *stabs him.*]
　　　　　　　　　　Caesar, thou art revenged,
　　　Even with the sword that killed thee.

　　　　　[*Dies.*]

PINDARUS
　　　So, I am free; yet would not so have been,
　　　Durst I have done my will. O Cassius!
50　　Far from this country Pindarus shall run,
　　　Where never Roman shall take note of him.

　　　　　[*Exit.*]

　　　　　Enter TITINIUS *and* MESSALA.

MESSALA
　　　It is but change, Titinius; for Octavius
　　　Is overthrown by noble Brutus's power,
　　　As Cassius's legions are by Antony.

TITINIUS
55　　These tidings will well comfort Cassius.

MESSALA
　　　Where did you leave him?

TITINIUS
　　　　　　　　　　　　All **disconsolate**,
　　　With Pindarus his bondman, on this hill.

MESSALA
　　　Is not that he that lies upon the ground?

TITINIUS
60　　He lies not like the living. O my heart!

MESSALA
　　　Is not that he?

TITINIUS
　　　　　　　　No, this was he, Messala,
　　　But Cassius is no more. O setting sun,
　　　As in thy red rays thou dost sink to night,
65　　So in his red blood Cassius's day is set.

thrust with the sword.   45

    PINDARUS *stabs him.*

Caesar, you've been revenged,
and by the same sword that killed you.

    He dies.

PINDARUS
    Now I am free—but I wouldn't have been
    if I had dared to do what I had wished. Oh, Cassius!
    Pindarus will run far away from this country,   50
    where no Roman will ever notice him.

    He exits. TITINIUS *and* MESSALA *enter.*

MESSALA
    We've only traded luck, Titinius—for Octavius
    has been defeated by noble Brutus's army,
    while Cassius's troops have been defeated by Antony.

TITINIUS
    This news will give good comfort to Cassius.   55

MESSALA
    Where did you leave him?

TITINIUS
    Completely hopeless
    on this hill, with his slave Pindarus.

MESSALA
    Isn't that he lying on the ground?

TITINIUS
    He doesn't lie there as if he were alive. Oh, my heart!   60

MESSALA
    Isn't it he?

TITINIUS
    No, it was he, Messala,
    but Cassius is no more. Oh, setting sun—
    just as you sink into red rays as night approaches,
    so Cassius's day has set in his red blood.   65

The sun of Rome is set. Our day is gone;
Clouds, dews, and dangers come; our deeds are done.
Mistrust of my success hath done this deed.

MESSALA

Mistrust of good success hath done this deed.
70   O hateful error, melancholy's child,*
Why dost thou show to the apt thoughts of men
The things that are not? O error, soon conceived,
Thou never com'st unto a happy birth,
But kill'st the mother that **engend'red** thee.

TITINIUS

75   What, Pindarus! Where are thou, Pindarus?

MESSALA

Seek him, Titinius, whilst I go to meet
The noble Brutus, thrusting this report
Into his ears. I may say "thrusting it,"
For piercing steel and darts envenomed
80   Shall be as welcome to the ears of Brutus
As tidings of this sight.

TITINIUS

               Hie you, Messala,
And I will seek for Pindarus the while.

[*Exit* MESSALA.]

Why didst thou send me forth, brave Cassius?
85   Did I not meet thy friends, and did not they
Put on my brows this wreath of victory,
And bid me give it thee? Didst thou not hear their shouts?
Alas, thou hast **misconstrued** everything.*
But hold thee, take this garland on thy brow;

---

70   *error, melancholy's child*   a fanciful genealogy intended to connect Cassius's death
with his gloomy, fatalistic mood. These formal, elaborate personifications occur
frequently in *Julius Caesar*, and they are used to make an allegorical comparison.

88   *misconstrued everything*   Cassius has completely misunderstood what happened
with Titinius earlier in this scene. As Titinius explains the events to us, he was

The sun of Rome has set. Our day has passed;
clouds, dews, and dangers are on their way. Our deeds are
  behind us.
His fear for the success of my mission made him do this.

MESSALA

His fear for the success of the battle made him do this.
Oh, hateful error, melancholy's child,   70
why do you show things that aren't real
to men's easily impressed minds? Oh, error, although you're
  quickly conceived,
your birth is never happy,
for you kill the mother who bore you!

TITINIUS

Pindarus! Where are you, Pindarus?   75

MESSALA

Look for him, Titinius, while I go meet
the noble Brutus and thrust this news
into his ears. I'm right to say "thrust it,"
for piercing blades and poisoned darts
would be as welcome to Brutus's ears   80
as news of this sight.

TITINIUS

Hurry, Messala.
Meanwhile, I'll look for Pindarus.

       MESSALA *exits.*

Why did you send me out, brave Cassius?
Didn't I meet your friends, and didn't they   85
put this wreath of victory on my head
and tell me to give it to you? Didn't you hear their shouts?
Alas, you misunderstood everything.
But wait a moment—wear this wreath on your head.

---

welcomed by the troops of Brutus, who had won a victory over Octavius.
The report that Pindarus gives Cassius from his lookout post is, of course,
misleading, especially the information that Titinius is taken. Cassius should have
verified this intelligence rather than committing suicide in despair. A sense of
fatality hangs over the conspirators, even when they are temporarily victorious
(as Brutus is over Octavius).

90　Thy Brutus bid me give it thee, and I
Will do his bidding.—Brutus, come apace,
And see how I regarded Caius Cassius.—
By your leave, gods. This is a Roman's part.*
Come, Cassius's sword, and find Titinius's heart.

> *Dies.*

> *Alarum. Enter* BRUTUS, MESSALA, YOUNG CATO,
> STRATO, VOLUMNIUS, *and* LUCILIUS, [*with* LABIO,
> FLAVIUS, *and others*].

BRUTUS

95　Where, where, Messala, doth his body lie?

MESSALA

Lo, yonder, and Titinius mourning it.

BRUTUS

Titinius's face is upward.

CATO

He is slain.

BRUTUS

O Julius Caesar, thou art mighty yet!
100　Thy spirit walks abroad and turns our swords
In our own proper entrails.

> *Low alarums.*

CATO

Brave Titinius!
Look whe'er he have not crowned dead Cassius.

BRUTUS

Are yet two Romans living such as these?
105　The last of all the Romans, fare thee well.
It is impossible that ever Rome
Should breed thy fellow.—Friends, I owe more tears
To this dead man than you shall see me pay.—
I shall find time, Cassius; I shall find time.—
110　Come, therefore, and to Thasos send his body.

93　*Roman's part*　The Roman view of suicide as a praiseworthy act, especially when
it is done to avoid dishonor, is directly opposed to the Christian condemnation
of suicide as a form of murder.

He puts the wreath on CASSIUS'S *head.*

Your Brutus told me to give it to you, and I   90
will do as he asked. Brutus, come here quickly
and see how I've honored Caius Cassius.
Gods, with your permission, I'll do my duty as a Roman.
Cassius's sword, come here, and find Titinius's heart!

> *He stabs himself with Cassius's sword and dies. Drums and*
> *trumpets.* BRUTUS, MESSALA, YOUNG CATO, STRATO,
> VOLUMNIUS, LUCILIUS, LABIO, *and* FLAVIUS *enter.*

BRUTUS

Where, where does his body lie, Messala?   95

MESSALA

Look, over there—and Titinius is mourning it.

BRUTUS

But Titinius's face is turned upward.

CATO.

He is dead.

BRUTUS

Oh, Julius Caesar, you are still mighty.
Your spirit walks through the world and turns our swords   100
into our own bodies.

> *Distant drums and trumpets.*

CATO

Brave Titinius!
Look at how he's crowned the dead Cassius.

BRUTUS

Are there still two Romans living like these men?
(*to the dead* CASSIUS) The last of all true Romans, farewell.   105
It is impossible that Rome
will ever breed your equals.—Friends, I owe more tears
to this dead man than you will see me shed.—
I shall find time, Cassius; I shall find time.—
And so, let's go and take his body to Thasos.   110

His funerals shall not be in our camp,
Lest it discomfort us. Lucilius, come;
And come, young Cato; let us to the field.—
Labio and Flavio set our battles on.
115 'Tis three a clock; and, Romans, yet ere night
We shall try fortune in a second fight.

    Exeunt.

We'll not hold his funeral in our camp,
for it might dishearten our soldiers.—Lucilius, come along.—
You, too, young Cato. Let us go to the field.—
Labio and Flavius, give our armies the command to march.
It's three o'clock; and Romans, before nightfall   115
we shall test fortune in a second fight.

    They exit.

ACT V, SCENE IV

[*Another part of the field.*] *Alarum. Enter* BRUTUS,
MESSALA, [YOUNG] CATO, LUCILIUS, *and*
FLAVIUS.

BRUTUS
Yet, countrymen, O yet hold up your heads!

[*Exit, with* MESSALA *and* FLAVIUS.]

[YOUNG] CATO
What bastard doth not? Who will go with me?
I will proclaim my name about the field.
I am the son of Marcus Cato,* ho!
5   A foe to tyrants, and my country's friend.
I am the son of Marcus Cato, ho!

Enter SOLDIERS *and fight.*

LUCILIUS
And I am Brutus, Marcus Brutus, I!
Brutus, my country's friend! Know me for Brutus!

[YOUNG CATO *is slain.*]

O young and noble Cato, art thou down?
10   Why, now thou diest as bravely as Titinius,
And mayst be honored, being Cato's son.

[FIRST] SOLDIER [*seizing* LUCILIUS]
Yield, or thou diest.

LUCILIUS
                                Only I yield to die.
There is so much that thou wilt kill me straight.

[*Offers money.*]

15   Kill Brutus and be honored in his death.

[FIRST] SOLDIER
We must not; a noble prisoner!

Enter ANTONY.

---

4   *Marcus Cato*   Young Cato is the brother of Portia, Brutus's wife.

ACT 5, SCENE 4

The field of battle. Drums and trumpets. BRUTUS, MESSALA, YOUNG CATO, LUCILIUS, *and* FLAVIUS *enter.*

BRUTUS
Countrymen, keep holding up your heads!

He exits with followers.

CATO
Who is so lowborn that he wouldn't do so? Who will go with me?
I will shout my name throughout the field.
Look, I am the son of Marcus Cato!
I'm a foe to tyrants and my country's friend.   5
Look, I am the son of Marcus Cato!

SOLDIERS enter and fight.

LUCILIUS (*impersonating* Brutus)
And I am Brutus—I am Marcus Brutus!
Brutus, my country's friend! Know that I am Brutus.

YOUNG CATO is killed.

Oh, young and noble Cato, have you fallen?
Why, you've died as bravely as Titinius did,   10
and you should be honored just as much, since you are Cato's son.

FIRST SOLDIER (*seizing* LUCILIUS)
Surrender or you die.

LUCILIUS
I only surrender so that I may die.
You'll get all this if you kill me immediately.

He offers money.

Kill Brutus and be praised for his death.   15

FIRST SOLDIER
We must not. He's a noble prisoner!

ANTONY enters.

SECOND SOLDIER

Room, ho! Tell Antony Brutus is ta'en.

FIRST SOLDIER

I'll tell the news. Here comes the General.—
Brutus is ta'en, Brutus is ta'en, my lord.

ANTONY

20   Where is he?

LUCILIUS

Safe, Antony; Brutus is safe enough.
I dare assure thee that no enemy
Shall ever take alive the noble Brutus.
The gods defend him from so great a shame.
25   When you do find him, or alive or dead,
He will be found like Brutus, like himself.

ANTONY

This is not Brutus, friend; but, I assure you,
A prize no less in worth. Keep this man safe;
Give him all kindness. I had rather have
30   Such men my friends than enemies. Go on,
And see whe'r Brutus be alive or dead;
And bring us word unto Octavius's tent
How everything is chanced.

     Exeunt.

SECOND SOLDIER
Make room. Tell Antony that Brutus has been captured.

FIRST SOLDIER
I'll tell him the news. Here comes the General.—
Brutus has been taken, Brutus has been taken, my lord.

ANTONY
Where is he?   20

LUCILIUS
Safe, Antony; Brutus is safe enough.
I dare to assure you that no enemy
will ever take the noble Brutus alive.
May the gods defend him from so great a shame!
Whenever you do find him—whether he's alive or dead—   25
Brutus will behave according to his own noble nature.

ANTONY
This is not Brutus, friend; but I assure you,
he's just as valuable a prize. Keep this man safe.
Treat him very kindly. I would rather have
such men as my friends than enemies. Go on,   30
and see whether Brutus is alive or dead,
and bring word to us in Octavius's tent
how everything has turned out.

They exit in different directions.

ACT V, SCENE V

[*Another part of the field.*] *Enter* BRUTUS,
DARDANUS, CLITUS, STRATO, *and* VOLUMNIUS.

BRUTUS
Come, poor remains of friends, rest on this rock.

CLITUS
Statilius showed the torchlight; but, my lord,
He came not back. He is or ta'en or slain.*

BRUTUS
Sit thee down, Clitus. Slaying is the word;
5   It is a deed in fashion. Hark thee, Clitus.

    [*Whispers.*]

CLITUS
What, I, my lord? No, not for all the world.

BRUTUS
Peace then, no words.

CLITUS
               I'll rather kill myself.

BRUTUS
Hark thee, Dardanus.

    [*Whispers.*]

DARDANUS
10   Shall I do such a deed?

CLITUS
O Dardanus!

DARDANUS!
O Clitus!

---

3   *slain* Plutarch relates that Statilius, as scout, went through the enemy's lines to
Cassius's camp and gave a prearranged signal by torchlight that all was well. He
was, however, slain on his way back to Brutus.

ACT 5, SCENE 5

The field of battle. BRUTUS, DARDANUS, CLITUS, STRATO, *and* VOLUMNIUS *enter.*

BRUTUS
Come here, you wretched, surviving friends; rest on this rock.

He sits down.

CLITUS
Statilius signaled us by torchlight; but, my lord,
he didn't come back. He's been taken or killed.

BRUTUS
Sit down, Clitus. Killing is the word for what happened to him;
it's a common deed these days. Listen, Clitus. 5

He whispers to CLITUS.

CLITUS
What—I, my lord? No, not for the whole world.

BRUTUS
Quiet, then, and say nothing.

CLITUS
I'd rather kill myself.

BRUTUS
Listen, Dardanus.

He whispers to DARDANUS.

DARDANUS
Could I do such a deed? 10

CLITUS
Oh, Dardanus!

DARDANUS
Oh, Clitus!

DARDANUS *and* CLITUS *step aside.*

CLITUS

What ill request did Brutus make to thee?

DARDANUS

To kill him, Clitus. Look, he meditates.

CLITUS

15   Now is that noble vessel full of grief,
That it runs over even at his eyes.

BRUTUS

Come hither, good Volumnius. List a word.

VOLUMNIUS

What says my lord?

BRUTUS

                    Why this, Volumnius:
20   The ghost of Caesar hath appeared to me
Two several times by night—at Sardis once
And this last night here in Philippi fields.
I know my hour is come.

VOLUMNIUS

                  Not so, my lord.

BRUTUS

25   Nay, I am sure it is, Volumnius.
Thou seest the world, Volumnius, how it goes;
Our enemies have beat us to the pit.

    Low alarums.

It is more worthy to leap in ourselves
Than tarry till they push us. Good Volumnius,
30   Thou know'st that we two went to school together.
Even for that our love of old, I prithee
Hold thou my swordhilts whilst I run on it.

VOLUMNIUS

That's not an office for a friend, my lord.

    Alarum still.

CLITUS

Fly, fly, my lord, there is no tarrying here.

CLITUS

What evil thing did Brutus request of you?

DARDANUS

To kill him, Clitus. Look, he's thinking.

CLITUS

That noble body is now so full of grief   15
that his tears run out through his eyes.

BRUTUS

Come here, good Volumnius. Hear just a word.

VOLUMNIUS

What does my lord have to say?

BRUTUS

Why, this, Volumnius: 20
The ghost of Caesar has appeared to me
two different times at night—once at Sardis,
and tonight here in the fields of Philippi.
I know that the hour of my death has come.

VOLUMNIUS.

That's not true, my lord.

BRUTUS

No, I am sure it is, Volumnius.   25
You see how things are, Volumnius.
Our enemies have driven us to our graves.

    Distant drums and trumpets.

It is nobler to leap in ourselves
than to wait until they push us. Good Volumnius,
you know that we two went to school together;   30
out of respect for our old friendship, I beg you
to hold my sword by its hilt while I run myself through with it.

VOLUMNIUS

That's no duty for a friend, my lord.

    Drums and trumpets continue.

CLITUS

Flee, flee, my lord! We can't stay here.

BRUTUS

35 Farewell to you—and you—and you, Volumnius.—
Strato, thou hast been all this while asleep.
Farewell to thee too, Strato.—Countrymen,
My heart doth joy that yet in all my life
I found no man but he was true to me.

40 I shall have glory by this losing day
More than Octavius and Mark Antony
By this vile conquest shall attain unto.
So fare you well at once; for Brutus's tongue
Hath almost ended his life's history.

45 Night hangs upon mine eyes; my bones would rest,
That have but labored to attain this hour.

Alarum. Cry within, "Fly, fly, fly!"

CLITUS
Fly, my lord, fly!

BRUTUS
                    Hence! I will follow.

[*Exeunt* CLITUS, DARDANUS, *and* VOLUMNIUS.]

I prithee, Strato, stay thou by the lord.
50 Thou art a fellow of a good respect;
Thy life hath had some smatch of honor in it.
Hold then my sword, and turn away thy face,
While I do run upon it. Wilt thou, Strato?

STRATO
Give me your hand first. Fare you well, my lord.

BRUTUS
55 Farewell, good Strato.

[*Runs on his sword.*]

Caesar, now be still.
I killed not thee with half so good a will.

Dies.

Alarum. Retreat. Enter ANTONY, OCTAVIUS,
MESSALA, LUCILIUS, *and the* ARMY.

BRUTUS

Farewell to you—and you—and you, Volumnius.— 35
Strato, you've been asleep this whole time.
Farewell to you, too, Strato.—Countrymen,
my heart rejoices that, in my whole life,
I've never found a man who wasn't loyal to me.
I will gain more glory by losing today 40
than Octavius and Mark Antony
will gain by winning their unjust cause.
So I say farewell right now, for Brutus's tongue
has almost finished telling his life's story.
Night covers my eyes; my bones want to rest, 45
for they have worked hard only to arrive at this moment of death.

> *Drums and trumpets. Offstage voices cry, "Flee, flee, flee!"*

CLITUS

Flee, my lord, flee!

BRUTUS

Go on. I will follow you.

> *All exit except* BRUTUS *and* STRATO.

Strato, I beg you to stay by your lord.
You are a fellow with a good reputation; 50
your life has had a taste of honor to it.
So hold my sword, and turn away your face
while I run onto it. Will you, Strato?

STRATO

Give me your hand first. Farewell, my lord.

BRUTUS

Farewell, good Strato. 55

> BRUTUS *runs on his sword.*

Caesar, rest peacefully now.
I didn't kill you half so eagerly.

> *He dies. Drums and trumpets, sounding a retreat.* ANTONY,
> OCTAVIUS, MESSALA, LUCILIUS, *and the* ARMY *enter.*

OCTAVIUS

What man is that?

MESSALA

My master's man.—Strato, where is thy master?

STRATO

60 Free from the bondage you are in, Messala.
The conquerors can but make a fire of him;
For Brutus only overcame himself,
And no man else hath honor by his death.

LUCILIUS

So Brutus should be found. I thank thee, Brutus,
65 That thou hast proved Lucilius's saying true.

OCTAVIUS

All that served Brutus, I will entertain them.—
Fellow, wilt thou bestow thy time with me?

STRATO

Ay, if Messala will prefer me to you.

OCTAVIUS

Do so, good Messala.

MESSALA

70 How died my master, Strato?

STRATO

I held the sword, and he did run on it.

MESSALA

Octavius, then take him to follow thee,
That did the latest service to my master.

ANTONY

This was the noblest Roman of them all.
75 All the conspirators save only he
Did that they did in envy of great Caesar;
He only, in a general honest thought
And common good to all, made one of them.
His life was gentle, and the elements
80 So mixed in him that nature might stand up
And say to all the world, "This was a man!"

OCTAVIUS
Who is that man?

MESSALA
My master's servant.—Strato, where is your master?

STRATO
Not taken prisoner like you, Messala.   60
The conquerors can only cremate his body, not capture him alive,
for Brutus alone conquered himself,
and no other man has won honor by his death.

LUCILIUS
This is how Brutus should be found. I thank you, Brutus,
for having proved true what Lucilius said about you.   65

OCTAVIUS
I will take everyone who served Brutus into my service.—
Fellow, will you devote your time to me?

STRATO
Yes, if Messala will recommend me to you.

OCTAVIUS
Do so, good Messala.

MESSALA
How did my master die, Strato?   70

STRATO
I held the sword, and he ran onto it.

MESSALA
Then take him as your servant, Octavius,
for he did the last service for my master.

ANTONY (*speaking a formal eulogy for the dead* BRUTUS)
This was the noblest Roman of them all.
All the conspirators except he   75
did what they did out of hatred for great Caesar.
He joined them only for impersonal reasons
and out of concern for the good of all.
His life was noble, and the elements
were so well-balanced in him that nature might stand up   80
and say to all the world, "This was a man."

OCTAVIUS
    According to his virtue let us use him,
    With all respect and rites of burial.
    Within my tent his bones tonight shall lie,
85   Most like a soldier, ordered honorably.
    So call the field to rest, and let's away
    To part the glories of this happy day.

      Exeunt omnes.

OCTAVIUS
　　Because of his excellence, let's treat him
　　with respect and give him full burial rites.
　　Tonight his bones will lie inside my tent,
　　for as a soldier, he deserves to be treated with honor.　　85
　　Order the army to rest, and let's go somewhere
　　to share the glories of this happy day.

　　　　They all exit.

Act V Review

Discussion Questions

1. How does Antony appear in Scene i?

2. What is accomplished during the parley between the two sides in Scene i?

3. In Scene i, what does Cassius tell Messala about his earlier philosophy? Explain how his viewpoint has changed.

4. Toward the end of the play, do you think Cassius would still say to Brutus, "The fault, dear Brutus, is not in our stars, / But in ourselves, that we are underlings" (Scene ii, lines 147–148)?

5. Why is suicide a difficult decision for Brutus?

6. At the time of his death, how does Brutus feel about his fortunes, as compared with those of the victors against him?

7. What are your final impressions of Brutus?

8. How is Octavius characterized in this play?

Literary Elements

1. Good drama has **conflict**: struggle between opposing forces. Look at Scene i, when the four generals meet for their battle parley. Name some things that increase the tension in this scene.

2. **Personification** means attributing human characteristics to nonhuman things. Explain how "error" is personified in Scene iii, and explore what Shakespeare gains by using this figure of speech.

3. **Mood**, or atmosphere, refers to the feelings the audience has toward the events of the play. For each of the scenes in Act V, try to pinpoint the mood and explain what language and images support your opinion.

4. What **double entendre**, or double meaning, is present in Brutus's words in Scene v, line 27: "Our enemies have beat us to the pit"?

Writing Prompts

1. Many people consider suicide a sin or a crime. But for Titinius and Cassius, it was a noble way to end life. Discuss the reasons why these characters, as well as other people, consider suicide noble. Make a list of these situations (an example might be "defeat"). Now imagine that you had a chance to talk to a person in this situation. Write what you would say and what alternative you might offer.

2. Write the victory speech that Antony or Octavius might make to the Roman people after their victory at the battle of Philippi.

3. The Roman army was famous for its organization, discipline, and courage. Research some aspect of the Roman legions—their makeup, weapons, or tactics, for example—and write a report on what you find.

4. Brutus has been torn between his loyalties to his friend and leader—Caesar—and his loyalties to the Roman Republic and the values it stands for. To what people, beliefs, groups, or organizations do you feel strongly loyal? Write your response in a short essay. Include specific details, examples, and anecdotes that will help others understand your perspective. If you have trouble deciding your priorities, explain why you think that is.

The Play in Review

Discussion and Analysis

1. Why do you think Shakespeare gives Caesar so few lines and so little stage time, even during the scenes in which he appears?

2. How are the common people portrayed in *Julius Caesar*? Discuss what the play seems to say about democracy.

3. In Orson Welles' "modern dress" production of *Julius Caesar*, some actors wore black uniforms like those of European dictators in the 1930s. What parallels do you see between the plot of *Julius Caesar* and politics today?

4. Stoicism is a philosophy that promotes a detached, fatalistic view of one's own life. It holds that one should endure with detachment and a tranquil heart both the pleasures and pains dealt out by fate. Trace how this Stoic philosophy affects Brutus's behavior and decisions throughout the play.

5. The conspirator Brutus believed that the immoral act of murder would in this case benefit all Romans. Do you agree that a noble end sometimes justifies less than noble means? Explain.

6. Judging from the play, how do you think the roles of married men and women have changed since Roman times?

7. In your opinion, was the friendship of Brutus and Cassius deep and true, or were they just using each other for help in overthrowing Caesar? Defend your position.

LITERARY ELEMENTS

1. In *Julius Caesar*, Shakespeare uses great insight to show the contrast between how **characters** see themselves and how they really are. Describe these different versions using a two-column chart. Do you notice a similar contrast in people you know?

2. As you might expect, this play about political beliefs and war is full of **conflict**. Name some ways in which Shakespeare increases the conflict via character personalities, relationships, language, and other plot devices.

3. Which **themes**, or main ideas, do you find most important in the play? Choose one and use evidence from the play to explore what Shakespeare might have believed about this idea.

4. In *Julius Caesar*, Shakespeare often played on **imagery**—vivid sensory description—related to the sky. Find such examples and discuss how they contribute to the play.

5. Where do you believe the **climax**, or emotional high point, is in this play? Explain what you think Shakespeare may have intended by placing the climax here.

6. *Rome* is often referred to in the play as a living person. Find an example of the **personification** of Rome and discuss how it adds to the play's meaning.

WRITING PROMPTS

1. Suppose the attempt on Caesar's life failed. Invent a new conclusion to the play *Julius Caesar* that shows what might have happened if Caesar had survived the attack at the Forum. Go back into the play as far as necessary to create a different ending. Write your new ending in play form.

2. Antony calls Brutus "the noblest Roman of them all." Decide what qualities or behavior make a person noble. Then apply your definition to Brutus, Cassius, and Caesar. Which of the three men do you consider the noblest? Explain your decision in an essay.

3. Write a description of your favorite character from the play. Use evidence from the play to support your opinions about this character and make clear why this person appeals to you.

4. If a Roman citizen had been asked to identify his or her greatest hero, many would have named a victorious general. How would you answer this question? Identify a personal hero or someone you admire. You might choose a political or religious leader, educator, author, or someone else, such as a family member, who has set an example you want to follow. In a short essay, tell about your hero's accomplishment or things about him or her that impress you. Would you want to be like this person? Explain why or why not.

5. Although Caesar dies in Act III, Shakespeare titled his play *Julius Caesar*. Read the following statements, and pick the one you most strongly agree with. Defend your argument with examples from the text.

    a. Shakespeare's title is good. Julius Caesar is a main character in this play.
    b. The title *Julius Caesar* is a weak one. A better title could be found for this play. (Suggest one, and give reasons for your choice.)

6. Pretend that the relationships between men and women in Roman times were similar to how they are today. Rewrite the dialogue between either Brutus and Portia or Caesar and Calphurnia. Show how the outcome of the play might be very different if the input of women were respected.

Multimodal and Group Activities

1. A book cover should invite you to read the book. Design your own cover for *Julius Caesar*. Then share your cover with the class. Discuss what type of reader will find it appealing.

2. Imagine that Brutus and his co-conspirators are going to be tried for Caesar's assassination. Prepare a mock trial for your class.

    Appoint students to be Brutus, his coconspirators, the judge, prosecution and defense lawyers, and witnesses. The rest of the class can serve as the jury. The trial should take into account the arguments that justify or excuse the actions of Brutus and his co-conspirators as well as the points the prosecution might make to prove their actions cannot be justified.

3. Pretend you are the casting director for a new production of *Julius Caesar*. Choose modern actors for the main characters, thinking carefully about why an actor fits a character in the play. You may then design a playbill or poster advertising your production, using imagery, typography, and language that gives the audience some idea of the way you will interpret this version.

4. Design costumes for some of the characters in *Julius Caesar*. Using the library and Internet, as well as other resources, look for pictures and descriptions of authentic clothing worn by men and women in Caesar's day. Examine the dress of commoners, aristocrats, and soldiers. You may sketch the garments or make replicas of the clothing for puppets or paper dolls. Or you may want to use illustrations using computer graphics or cartoon panels.

5. Find a work of art based on *Julius Caesar*, such as a musical piece, another play, or a painting. In an oral presentation to your group or class, explain how the music, drama, or art captures the mood and events of Shakespeare's play. You may need to use a VCR, boom box, or slides to share this work with your audience.

SHAKESPEARE'S LIFE

Many great authors can be imagined as living among the characters in their works. Historical records reveal how these writers spoke, felt, and thought. But Shakespeare is more mysterious. He never gave an interview or wrote an autobiography—not even one of his letters survives. What we know about his life can be told very briefly.

Shakespeare was born in April 1564. The exact date of his birth is unknown, but he was baptized on April 26 in the Stratford-upon-Avon church. His father, John, was a prominent local man who served as town chamberlain and mayor. Young William attended

grammar school in Stratford, where he would have learned Latin—a requirement for a professional career—and some Greek.

In 1582, William married Anne Hathaway. He was 18; she was 26. At the time of their marriage, Anne was already three months pregnant with their first daughter, Susanna. In 1585, the couple had twins, Judith and Hamnet. Hamnet died before reaching adulthood, leaving Shakespeare no male heir.

Even less is known about Shakespeare's life between 1585 and 1592. During that time, he moved to London and became an actor and playwright. He left his family behind in Stratford. Although he surely visited them occasionally, we have little evidence about what Shakespeare was like as a father and a husband.

Several of his early plays were written during this time, including *The Comedy of Errors*, *Titus Andronicus*, and the three parts of *Henry VI*. In those days, working in the theater was rather like acting in soap operas today—the results may be popular, but daytime series aren't recognized as serious art. In fact, many people were opposed to even allowing plays to be performed. Ministers warned their congregations of the dangers of going to plays.

But Shakespeare and his friends were lucky. Queen Elizabeth I loved plays. She protected acting companies from restrictive laws and gave them her permission to perform. Shakespeare wrote several plays to be performed for the queen, including *Twelfth Night*.

Queen Elizabeth I

After Elizabeth's death in 1603, Shakespeare's company became known as the King's Men. This group of actors performed for James I, who had ruled Scotland before becoming the King of England. Perhaps to thank James for his patronage, Shakespeare wrote *Macbeth*, which included two topics of strong interest to the king—Scottish royalty and witchcraft.

Unlike many theater people, Shakespeare actually earned a good living. By 1599, he was part owner of the Globe, one of the newest theaters in London. Such plays as *Othello*, *Hamlet*, and *King Lear* were first performed there.

In 1610 or 1611, Shakespeare moved back to the familiar surroundings of Stratford-upon-Avon. He was almost fifty years old, well past middle age by 17th-century standards. Over the years, he'd invested in property around Stratford, acquiring a comfortable estate and a family coat of arms.

But Shakespeare didn't give up writing. In 1611, his new play *The Tempest* was performed at court. In 1613, his play *Henry VIII* premiered. This performance was more dramatic than anyone expected. The stage directions called for a cannon to be fired when "King Henry" came on stage. The explosion set the stage on fire, and the entire theater burned to the ground.

Shakespeare died in 1616 at the age of 52. His gravestone carried this inscription:

> **Good friend for Jesus sake forbear**
> **To dig the dust enclosed here!**
> **Blest be the man that spares these stones,**
> **And curst be he that moves my bones.**

This little verse, so crude that it seems unlikely to be Shakespeare's, has intrigued countless scholars and biographers.

Anyone who loves Shakespeare's plays and poems wants to know more about their author. Was he a young man who loved Anne Whateley but was forced into a loveless marriage with another Anne? Did he teach school in Stratford, poach Sir Thomas Lucy's deer, or work for a lawyer in London? Who is the "dark lady" of his sonnets?

But perhaps we are fortunate in our ignorance. Orson Welles, who directed an all-black stage production of *Macbeth* in 1936, put it this way: "Luckily, we know almost nothing about Shakespeare . . . and that makes it so much easier to understand [his] works . . . It's an egocentric, romantic, 19th-century conception that the artist is more interesting and more important than his art."

In Shakespeare's world, there can be little question of which is truly important, the work or the author. Shakespeare rings up the curtain and then steps back into the wings, trusting the play to a cast of characters so stunningly vivid that they sometimes seem more real than life.

Shakespeare's Theater

In Shakespeare's London, a day's entertainment often began with a favorite amusement, bearbaiting. A bear would be captured and chained to a stake inside a pit. A pack of dogs would be released, and they would attack the bear. Spectators placed bets on which would die first. Admission to these pits cost only a penny, so they were very popular with working-class Londoners.

The Swan Theatre in London, drawn in 1596, the only known contemporary image of an Elizabethan theater interior

After the bearbaiting was over, another penny purchased admission to a play. Each theater had its own company of actors, often supported by a nobleman or a member of the royal family. For part of his career, Shakespeare was a member of the Lord

Chamberlain's Men. After the death of Queen Elizabeth I, King James I became the patron of Shakespeare's company. The actors became known as the King's Men.

As part owner of the Globe Theatre, Shakespeare wrote plays, hired actors, and paid the bills. Since the Globe presented a new play every three weeks, Shakespeare and his actors had little time to rehearse or polish their productions. To complicate matters even more, most actors played more than one part in a play.

Richard Tarleton, Elizabethan actor famous for his clowning

Boys played all the female roles. Most acting companies had three or four youths who were practically raised in the theater. They started acting as early as age seven and played female roles until they began shaving. Shakespeare had a favorite boy actor (probably named John Rice) who played Cleopatra and Lady Macbeth. Actresses would not become part of the English theater for another fifty years.

The audience crowded into the theater at about 2 p.m. The cheapest seats weren't seats at all but standing room in front of the stage. This area, known as the "pit," was occupied by "groundlings" or "penny knaves," who could be more trouble to the actors than they were worth. If the play was boring, the groundlings would throw rotten eggs or vegetables. They talked loudly to their friends, played cards, and even picked fights with each other. One theater was set on fire by audience members who didn't like the play.

The theater was open to the sky, so rain or snow presented a problem. However, the actors were partially protected by a roof known as the "heavens," and wealthier patrons sat in three stories of sheltered galleries that surrounded the pit and most of the main stage.

The main stage, about 25 feet deep and 45 feet wide, projected into the audience, so spectators were closely involved in the action. This stage was rather bare, with only a few pieces of furniture. But this simplicity allowed for flexible and fluid staging. Unlike too many later productions, plays at the Globe did not grind to a halt for scene changes. When one group of actors exited through one doorway and a new group entered through another, Shakespeare's audience understood that a new location was probably being represented.

Behind the main stage was the "tiring-house," where the actors changed costumes. Above the stage was a gallery that, when it wasn't occupied by musicians or wealthy patrons, could suggest any kind of high place—castle ramparts, a cliff, or a balcony.

Special effects were common. A trapdoor in the main stage allowed ghosts to appear. Even more spectacularly, supernatural beings could be lowered from above the stage. For added realism, actors hid bags of pig's blood and guts under their stage doublets. When pierced with a sword, the bags spilled out over the stage and produced a gory effect.

All these staging methods and design elements greatly appealed to Elizabethan audiences and made plays increasingly popular. By the time Shakespeare died in 1616, there were more than thirty theaters in and around London.

What would Shakespeare, so accustomed to the rough-and-tumble stagecraft of the Globe, think of the theaters where his plays are performed today? He would probably miss some of the vitality of the Globe. For centuries now, his plays have been most often performed on stages with a frame called the "proscenium arch," which cleanly separates the audience from the performers. This barrier tends to cast a peculiar shroud of privacy over his plays so that his characters do not seem to quite enter our world.

But with greater and greater frequency, Shakespeare's plays are being performed outdoors or in theaters with three- or four-sided stages. And a replica of the Globe Theatre itself opened in London in 1996, only about 200 yards from the site of the original. This

The new Globe Theatre, London

new Globe is an exciting laboratory where directors and actors can test ideas about Elizabethan staging. Their experiments may change our ideas about how Shakespeare's plays were performed and give new insights into their meaning.

THE GLOBE THEATRE

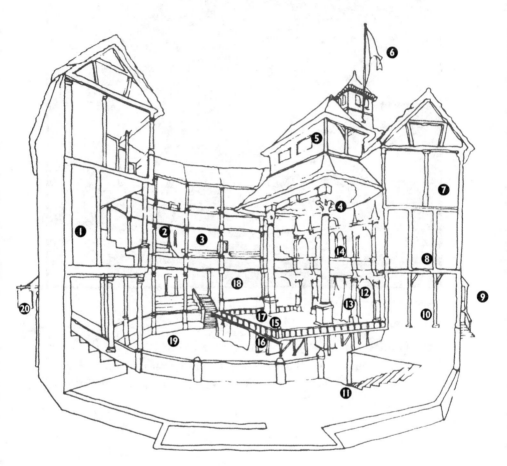

1 **Corridor** A passageway serving the middle gallery.

2 **Entrance** Point leading to the staircase and upper galleries.

3 **Middle Gallery** The seats here were higher priced.

4 **The Heavens** So identified by being painted with the zodiac signs.

5 **Hut** A storage area that also held a winch system for lowering characters to the stage.

6 **Flag** A white flag above the theater meant a show that day.

7 **Wardrobe** A storage area for costumes and props.

8 **Dressing Rooms** Rooms where actors were "attired" and awaited their cues.

9 **Tiring-House Door** The rear entrance or "stage door" for actors or privileged spectators.

10 **Tiring-House** Backstage area providing space for storage and costume changes.

11 **Stairs** Theatergoers reached the galleries by staircases enclosed by stairwells.

12 **Stage Doors** Doors opening into the Tiring-House.

13 **Inner Stage** A recessed playing area often curtained off except as needed.

14 **Gallery** Located above the stage to house musicians or spectators.

15 **Trapdoor** Leading to the "Hell" area, where a winch elevator was located.

16 **Hell** The area under the stage, used for ghostly comings and goings or for storage.

17 **Stage** Major playing area jutting into the Pit, creating a sense of intimacy.

18 **Lords Rooms** or private galleries. Six pennies let a viewer sit here, or sometimes on stage.

19 **The Pit** Sometimes referred to as "The Yard," where the "groundlings" watched.

20 **Main Entrance** Here the doorkeeper collected admission.

IMAGE CREDITS